CHURCH THROUGH THE ROOF:
Re-Storying Your Church's Ministry

Alvin C. Bernstine

Copyright © 2016. Alvin C. Bernstine

ISBN: 978-0-9767020-3-0

TABLE OF CONTENTS

Acknowledgments v

Foreword vi

Preface vii

Chapter 1
    The Concept 1

Chapter 2
    The Context 9

Chapter 3
    Jesus in the House 19

Chapter 4
    On Being Welcoming and Accepting 28

Chapter 5
    Preaching and Teaching a Healing Word 38

Chapter 6
    Compassion 45

Chapter 7
    Collaboration 54

Chapter 8
    Creativity 63

Chapter 9
    Conflict 71

Chapter 10
    Change 79

Chapter 11
    Commission 88

Chapter 12
    Celebration 95

Addendum
    BMBC Core Values 103

    The Discipleship Process Wheel 105

    The 5 Stages of Spiritual Growth 106

ACKNOWLEDGMENTS

I want to express my appreciation to one of my dearest friends in life and ministry: Presiding Bishop of the Full Gospel Baptist Fellowship, Dr. Joseph Warren Walker III. During a recent leadership conference, God used him to speak this book into existence. He referenced the foundational text of this book in a sermonic presentation and cited the essential ideas that I am attempting to expound upon. His hermeneutical genius and pastoral practicality stirred within me the incentive to pursue his thoughts. If the following words are helpful to anyone, he is to get the credit. If my thoughts confuse, then I misinterpreted what I don't want to misrepresent—the wisdom of my beloved friend.

Special thanks to Bethlehem Missionary Baptist Church for trusting me on this journey of re-storying our ministry. You are, indeed, "Church Through the Roof!" The cover design was created by one of our incredible members, Jessica Jones, a youthful witness of our re-storying journey. Special thanks to Reverend Shane Scott and the Macedonia Baptist Church of Los Angeles for entrusting me to test my theory during your leadership retreat. Joyce Evans provides an amazing ministry of creative design and typesetting.

FOREWORD

One of the critical challenges and essential components of any institution is to take an honest assessment of where it is and what direction it is heading. The church is no different. In order to remain viable and relevant it must embrace change and implement strategies that can prevent it from becoming an ecclesiastical relic of the past. I have watched the painful decline in membership and momentum in many churches across the world. There is a common denominator in them all. They were not open to positive change. They, in essence, lacked a transformative story.

What my friend Dr. Bernstine has done is carefully and skillfully exposed this problem as well as provided strategies to help churches recover from imminent social extinction. Change is difficult for us all yet is necessary to our growth and development. I've Pastored Mount Zion Baptist Church in Nashville for over 23 years and I've witnessed first hand the stressors that accompany change. Change threatens our way of doing things and causes us to revisit our level of commitment to the organization. I'm convinced that nobody wants to be a "once was" church. Dr. Bernstine has given us a masterpiece on how to remain vibrant and relevant while carrying out the mission of Jesus Christ in a Post-Modern context.

The challenges the church faces today are unlike anything we've seen in years. The church must recognize the need to be relevant and position itself programmatically and prophetically to be at the forefront of these issues. This is a tremendous opportunity for us all to sit at the feet of the brilliance of Alvin Bernstine and receive practical instruction on the creative art of doing church through the roof. Thank you my friend for this contribution to the Kingdom. I'm convinced we all will be better because you have put our heart and experience to pen and paper.

Bishop Joseph W. Walker, III
Presiding Bishop Full Gospel Baptist Church Fellowship
Senior Pastor Mount Zion Baptist Church, Nashville, TN

PREFACE

Years ago, we were invited by the musical genius George Benson to consider that "Everything Must Change." Anyone who listened to George Benson sing was melodically convinced that:

> Everything must change
> Nothing stays the same
> Everyone must change
> No one stays the same
>
> The young become the old
> And mysteries do unfold
> 'Cause that's the way of time
> Nothing and no one goes unchanged
>
> There are not many things in life
> You can be sure of
> Except rain comes from the clouds
> Sun lights up the sky
> And hummingbirds do fly
>
> Winter turns to spring
> A wounded heart will heal
> But never much too soon
> Yes, everything must change

Of interest is that church people were singing this song, but were going to their respective churches and assuming the position of another song, "I Shall Not Be Moved." In essence, we were celebrating a song of change, but living out a story without change. Since the year that song was sung, 1977, the world has changed exponentially. Even now, everything is undergoing change. In fact, most of the leadership in our churches comes from a generation of people born from that date forward; or at least most of us started leading after 1977. I've been serving as a pastor for over thirty years, beginning in 1984, seven years after the release of that song. My pastorate has extended across the years and across the country, dealing with three different congregations in three distinct parts of the country, all of which were resistant to change.

I have come to realize that the resistance was not so much to change, but the commitment to a story of themselves. Clearly, there was once a grand story to live out. It was filled with legends, and for the most part, unfulfilled promises. Unfortunately, the grand story of themselves had been fulfilled, and the current story had closed endings. Closed endings exist when the outcomes of the congregational story have been decided and there is no longer an evolving plot ascending to a tense and exciting climax. When characters are caught within stories of closed endings, the best they can do is participate in the drama of reruns. We can improvise, but we all know the conclusion has already been decided.

Too often, it is the story of closed endings that determines how congregations are packaged for the public's consideration. The stories of most congregations are packaged in narratives whose endings have been closed, predetermined by the histories in which they seem trapped to repeat, rehearse, and relive. There can be no question that the traditional church is declining. According to some statistics, church attendance has decreased in North America by 60 percent. In the African American community, once bourgeoning congregations have dwindled down to frighteningly scarce numbers. Many are like dinosaurs, massive institutions without the human sustenance to maintain a respectable existence. There are congregations in our communities whose numbers have become so meager that the basic maintenance of a pastor is a difficult undertaking. Some congregations have been embarrassed out of massive structures that started dwarfing its aging and declining membership. Sadder yet is the fact that young people are not likely to attend an old building filled with old people doing church in old ways, living out closed-ended stories.

> Closed endings exist when the outcomes of the congregational story have been decided and there is no longer an evolving plot ascending to a tense and exciting climax.

We are people of stories, and our stories, even church stories, need not be closed-ended. To be alive is to live out a story, and for our churches to come alive, we must continue to live out the gospel story, which is a living story.

Therefore, the primary need in most congregations is a dynamic and compelling story, inviting people into faithful living.

I believe a narrative theological perspective and the missional approach to ministry provide local congregations an opportunity to rethink, recalibrate, and resume responsible ministry by developing dynamic stories. The narrative theological perspective embraces God-talk with a view toward enlivening faith with stories. Likewise, the missional concept provides essential dynamics for the re-storying process.

Narrative theology boldly demystifies life-denying myths and promotes the life-giving faith of kerygma, which is story. Interestingly, the missional perspective accepts the death of Christendom while reimagining ways in which to engage the faith contextually. This represents a powerful and hopeful opportunity, because the goal is to enliven faith stories that are faithful to the particularities of a people's culture, history, and current context. While I'm theologically resistant to being a market-driven, consumer-based leader, there are some truths the marketplace has embraced that the church can ill-afford to ignore. The one truth we can ill-afford to ignore is that perception is everything. The attraction of Jesus was that "He taught as one with authority, not like the scribes." He did things no one had ever seen before, and said things in ways people had never heard. He promoted the same God of his tradition, but he didn't do it in traditional ways. He presented new life possibilities by promoting a vision of the Kingdom of God in the imaginative discourse of stories.

Mark Twain once said, "You can't depend on your eyes when your imagination is out of focus." The church seems to have become immune to imagination and has a failure to embrace the biblical assertion that "We walk by faith and not by sight." Faith is the imaginative impetus of the church's witness. Likewise, faith finds its most powerful expression in stories. Moreover, we must be diligent in how we are perceived, or we are likely to be self-deceived by what traditional eyes consider to be "the" church story, which is often closed-ended self-righteousness.

> Faith is the imaginative impetus of the church's witness.

The way a reality is perceived largely determines its fate. We, the church, must be diligent in how we are viewed in the world if we are to be effective in it. We can ill-afford to confine our faith in stories with closed endings. We are responsible for whether or not people meet Jesus, and we cannot abdicate our responsibility by being blindly attached to an ineffective story and image of who we are.

> Everything must change
> Nothing stays the same
> Everyone must change
> No one stays the same

1
THE CONCEPT

Years ago my preaching mentor and life tutor, the late Samuel Dewitt Proctor, was invited to Fisk University to serve as dean. The president of Fisk informed Dr. Proctor he was needed at Fisk University to provide the university "tone." A strange assignment for a dean, but what the president saw was a need for the university to possess a certain quality that would define its values, attitudes, and presuppositions. Dr. Proctor did not accept the assignment, but his sharing of the story with me describes something about what Church Through the Roof is all about. To all who knew anything about Dr. Samuel Dewitt Proctor, we knew he had the incredible capacity to encapsulate life in stories.

I want to share what has become one of the most rewarding experiences in my thirty-plus years as a pastor. Admittedly, I am in the closing stages of my pastoral journey, but my current experience has provided me with a perspective that has been vocationally invigorating. At this juncture in ministry, I believe I have been favored by God to tap into what is essential for enlivening a congregation toward meaningful ministry: shaping a ministry story worth living for. I further believe that every pastor and church leader wants to see his or her church being enlivened in responsible ministry. However, such will not come through mere good intentions or with a sanctified heart. Neither does responsible ministry come through casting a vision and developing thoughtful mission statements, as important as these tools might be. Yet these are the tools of what the psychologist Jerome Bruner identified as the "paradigmatic mode."[1] The paradigmatic mode is an attempt to comprehend the human experience in terms of tightly reasoned analyses, logical proof, and empirical observations.

After thirty-plus years of sometimes up and sometimes down, I have determined what our churches need are narratives that resonate throughout the congregation and invite people into their own adventure of living out the Christian story. I want to assert that Christian leadership happens through the creation of a ministry story so compelling, the congregation embraces it as its own. It is the other mode of thinking that Bruner identifies as the narrative

---

[1] Bruner, Jerome, *Acts of Meaning*, (Cambridge, MA: Harvard University Press, 1990).

mode, where the concern is with human wants and needs. We must become intentional about developing the kind of ministry tone that will reshape and recast the story of congregational life as the gospel, or God-story, impacts human wants and needs.

> Everything I've learned that has been helpful, hopeful, painful, and transformative has been through stories.

Everything I've learned that has been helpful, hopeful, painful, and transformative has been through stories. I learned how to read by reading stories. The stories I read, from the docile doings of *Dick and Jane* to the radical rawness of *Manchild in the Promised Land*, informed me of some invaluable truths about life. History was taught to me through stories. Although the sanitized versions of American history distorted and deceived, it was through other stories that I was able to re-story what was actual truth and demythologize that which was harmfully false.

When I consider the music that has informed and shaped my life, the most impactful songs were couched in stories. Recently, I removed from my playlist of songs a one-time favorite song, the Temptation's "Papa Was a Rolling Stone." Although I yet love the instrumental genius of the Funk Brothers, the lyrics of the song did not represent my father-family relationship. After listening closely to the lyrics, I decided I did not honor the legacy of my late father by embracing the song. My father-story was not a rolling stone, and wherever he hung his hat was not his home. He was a cornerstone, a man of integrity who was a man of the home. As an intergenerational pastor, I came to better understand the hip-hop generations because I understand that behind every song is a story. As a preacher, I witnessed the psalms come alive once I was able to attach the song to a story.

My primary and even current faith formations have been through the stories I was taught, heard preached, and those I now preach. In the African American community, a preacher's preaching has been communally validated when word gets out that he or she "can tell the story!" The Bible is encapsulated in stories, all of which are designed to shape faithful living, not to capture us within the closed-ended prisons of some oppressive literalism. How powerful an insight from Daniel Taylor when he writes:

Story is our best hope for flying over the chasms that separate individuals, races, genders, ages (and ages), cultures, classes, and the myriad other differences that render us unique (and potentially lonely). We are told many of these chasm-leaping stories in school. All the academic disciplines, and pre-eminently the humanities, are in the storytelling business.[2]

The idea of "story" is behind the popular marketing strategy of rebranding, or repackaging. In his book *The Power of Storytelling – Dominate the Market With Your Story,* Michael Pease says, "According to research, consumers who take a step to purchase your product or service are mainly driven by the likeability of your story."[3] To gain, or regain, a profitable share of the market, companies are known to rebrand themselves, or re-story their products with an open-ended narrative. When I listen to some pastors and denominational presentations, it seems we don't realize that "People forget statistics and facts, but they don't forget a good story…This is especially true if your story conveys a message related to the things your audience cares about deeply."[4] No wonder many companies have tapped into the power of conceptualizing a product into a narrative construct in which a lived experience can be imagined. Taco Bell promotes *Live Mas,* which is Spanish for "live more." A particular Taco Bell commercial never mentions a taco or a burrito, but the consumer is invited into a story of life. (I don't believe it a big stretch to suggest their storyline is borrowing from John 10:10, "I came that you might have life and have it more abundantly.")

Unlike Taco Bell, who minimizes their primary products, tacos and burritos, to invite us into an experience, we have an obligation to be faithful to the Christian faith. Our stories must possess theological integrity, and they work best when the story is framed in biblical imagery. We cannot ignore the fact that, as Dan McAdams says in *The Stories We Live By,* "Human experience is storied because of the way most of us comprehend such human actions as being organized in time."[5]

---

[2] Taylor, Daniel, *Tell Me a Story,* (Saint Paul, MN: Bog Walk Press, 2001), 12
[3] Pease, Michael, *The Power of Storytelling – Dominate the Market with Your Story,* loc. 8.
[4] Ibid., loc 21.
[5] McAdams, Dan P., *The Stories We Live By,* (New York, NY: The Guilford Press, 1993), 30

I believe the missional church advocates have provided the church an intriguing approach to ministry that theologically supports re-storying ministry with biblical integrity, and does so without being culturally insulting. Although best articulated by the Australian church, in North America, Ed Stetzer and Alan Hirsch have probably done more to spread missional ideas to the average local church planter and pastor than anyone else. Unlike many of the church growth models of the 80s and 90s, the missional perspective recaptures what is vital to biblical faith—the gospel story. Its commitment to the apostolic emphasis, a respect for the narrative value of cultural distinctions, and a serious critique of Christian colonialism constitutes, for me, a healthy theological framework for constructing healthy stories. The acknowledgment of the colonialism of the Christian faith is a huge admission and confession that the church's story has often been coopted by the closed-end narrative of empire. At its best, there is a prophetic tone to the missional approach, as it recognizes and respects the gospel story and not a mere imposition of marketing gimmicks for the sake of numbers. Michael Frost asserts:

> There is a prophetic tone to the missional approach, as it recognizes and respects the gospel story and not a mere imposition of marketing gimmicks for the sake of numbers.

> We are a story-formed community. The Christian experience is not primarily formed by our liturgy, doctrine, or ecclesiology, as important as those might be. We are formed by the dangerous stories of our great hero.[6]

As a proponent of the prophetic, I agree that, "One reason the civil rights movement has wandered in recent decades is that we have moved from 'I have a dream' to 'I have a program.' Martin Luther King told stories [while] current leaders cite statistics. Stories engage both the heart and the head and move people to action. Statistics elicit counter-statistics and move people to argue. Stories demand a response (that is, responsibility); statistics encourage a rebuttal."[7]

---

[6] Michael Frost, *Exiles: Living Missionally in a Post-Christian Culture*, (Peabody, MA: Hendrickson Publishers, Inc., 2006), 13.
[7] Ibid., 13.

As a struggling pastor of a local church, I have found Alan Hirsch and Dave Ferguson's[8] forthright presentation of the need for systemic change in the way we do church quite helpful. Bishop Joseph Walker III's *LeaderShift*, also provides an incredibly helpful perspective on leading a church to more relevant expressions of ministry.[9]

Walker's emphasis is on the importance of transitions, open-endedness, within a leader's life as being pivotal in facilitating a process by which the re-storying process takes place. By sharing his amazing journey in life and in ministry, he gives testimony to what Hirsch and Ferguson identify as Movementum. Bishop Walker embodies the Movementum potential for re-storying congregations trapped in closed-ended stories.

I believe what's taking place at my current ministry context, the Bethlehem Missionary Baptist Church, is Movementum. Without any prior knowledge of the missional perspective, we were facilitating our church in the process of Movementum. Furthermore, I find the images provided by Hirsch and Ferguson to be quite helpful in illustrating the process of re-storying our ministry.

The following is a morphed version of one presented by Hirsch and Ferguson

The above image is an attempt to illustrate and demonstrate our effort to use the biblical text as a means of determining what Jesus wants us to see

---

[8] Alan Hirsh and David Ferguson, *On the Verge: A Journey Into the Apostolic Future of the Church*, (Grand Rapids, MI: Zondervan Books, 2011).
[9] Joseph W. Walker III, *LeaderShifts: Mastering Transitions in Leadership & Life*, (Nashville, TN: Abingdon Press, 2014).

(imagine); to fully get it by understanding what He wants us to understand (shift); and to obey and do what He wants us to do (innovate). In essence, to participate in the gospel story is to see it, get it, and obediently do it. Good stories are imaginative invitations to consider life in a more hopeful manner, regardless of what obstacle(s) challenge or intrude upon it.

Last year, I befriended an amazing religious leader and spiritual healer, Estelle Frankel. Estelle is a psychotherapist who provides incredible leadership to a nontraditional Jewish congregation. (She is literally re-storying her faith community.) She visited Bethlehem one Sunday and heard me present a sermonic presentation on Church Through the Roof. She admitted not knowing what was meant by Church Through the Roof, but shared with me what she thought it meant, saying, "I didn't really know what Church Through the Roof meant. I was guessing that it had something to do with going beyond the limits of the ordinary, beyond the limits of the laws of nature."

> a call for the church to do church beyond the limits of the ordinary and to extend itself beyond the limits of any closed-ended assumptions by telling the story again.

Admittedly, her guess says more than my intentional framing. In a recent New Members' Orientation class, I shared the re-storying approach, and a twelve-year-old boy noted that what we were doing was "telling the story again." Isn't that what the Bible provides for us, a tool for telling the story again? Church Through the Roof is, indeed, a call for the church to do church beyond the limits of the ordinary and to extend itself beyond the limits of any closed-ended assumptions by telling the story again. No one can refute that the ministry of Jesus re-storied ordinary expressions of belief and catapulted his followers to live beyond the limits of closed-ended assumptions. To believe the gospel was to participate in life through the narrative, or kerygma, of a new story.

The following thoughts represent my humble attempts to experience the church in a way that moves us beyond the ordinary, with the hope of us following Jesus beyond the limits of traditional closed-ended assumptions about ministry. While story consists of certain "story grammar," Church Through the Roof consists of three irreplaceable realities and seven indispensable dynamics. We consider these realities and dynamics as being essential to our dynamic story. I capture these realities and dynamics in the Markan Pericope, a short story within the canonized life of Jesus. Those realities and dynamics are as follows:

THREE IRREPLACEABLE REALITIES

1. Jesus is in the house! (A pervasive Christology)
2. All people are welcomed and accepted! (An inclusive anthropology)
3. A healing word is preached and taught! (A therapeutic hermeneutic)

SEVEN INDISPENSABLE DYNAMICS

1. Compassion – the movement of the heart to erase the mistakes of competition.
2. Collaboration – relationally driven ministry with accountable expectations.
3. Creativity – allowing new ideas to reshape challenging circumstances.
4. Conflict – healthy approaches to inevitable challenges.
5. Change – the radical altering of assumed realities.
6. Commission – responsible engagement in God's mission.
7. Celebration – enjoying more of what we love to see.

QUESTIONS FOR GROUP DISCUSSION

1. Share your thoughts and reactions to a church being shaped by compelling ministry story versus being shaped by hierarchical structures and systems.

2. Share some memorable story in your life. This could be from life, movie, theatre, or book.

3. Identify some story-based realities in your community, such as those being used in marketing products.

4. What are your thoughts on Movementum?

5. What's in the way of your congregation, family, or organization creating a new story?

2

THE CONTEXT

TEXT: *And again He entered Capernaum after some days, it was heard He was in the house. Immediately many gathered together, so that there was no longer room to receive them, not even near the door. And He preached the word to them. (Mark 2:1–2, NKJV)*

Deacon Freddie Collier, who served with me in Nashville, appreciated my preaching when I would do what he called "walk heavy." Deacon's understanding of me "walking heavy" was to point out a faith challenge that was formidable, obvious, and candidly stated. I want to begin this journey by walking heavy. My heavy walking is on what I consider the obvious evolution of our relationship with God. There are three words in our text that could preface what I'm trying to communicate, and those words are, *"after some days."* After some days, there are things that ought to be obvious as we grow in our relationship with God. After some days, it ought to become obvious that the most important thing in your life, and in my life, is our relationship with God. After some days of spending time with God, it ought to become obvious to all who dare to see that there is nothing more important than our relationship with God.

Our faith is an experience lived in time and developed over time. A definition of story offered by Daniel Taylor is "The telling of the significant actions of characters over time."[10] We embody the actions of characters over time. There are some days in our Christian experience. Dan McAdams says, "Human time is a storied affair."[11] We start somewhere, but we also are going somewhere. There is an "after some days" to the lived experience of the Christian life. A provocative inquiry of ministry or congregational location is, "What got us here won't get us there."

After some days, I ought to be like the senior sister who loved God so much, she publically violated the King's English and declared, "God are good!" When the preacher tried to correct her and give her the right subject verb agreement, "God is good," she said, "That might work for you, but for me 'is' is not strong enough." The old woman had what the scholars call a high

---

[10] Taylor, 15.
[11] McAdams, 30.

theology, a high estimate of God. In other words, her love for God was through the roof.

Likewise, after some days of being nurtured in the environment of quality worship, my personal and communal worship ought to be through the roof. After some days of being encouraged to worship, I grow to understand that worship is my primary expression of demonstrating my love and adoration of God. I might not get it at first, but after some days, *"I will bless the Lord with all my soul."* After some days, *"I will make a joyful noise."* After some days, *"I will lift up holy hands and give God praise."* After some days, *"My soul cries out to the Lord,"* and my worship of God ought to go through the roof.

Yet it should be noted that when one's theology advances, one's ecclesiology ought to advance as well. In other words, when one's concept and appreciation of God grows, so ought one's concept and appreciation of God's church. If our love for God is through the roof, our way of being the church is through the roof. A viable theology is best articulated in the story of our experience with God. The story we are living out in God becomes an act of praise that takes us ecclesiastically through the roof.

After some days, serving the Lord becomes a priority. After some days, engaging my life in ministry becomes a priority. After some days, I see myself as being actively involved in the ministry of reconciliation. After some days, the world ought to know that I am a servant of the most-high God. Not the first day, but after some days, it becomes clear that I *"love the Lord with all my heart, with all my mind, and with all my might,"* and it is manifested in how I do church because church goes through the roof!

Let me walk heavy! I want to offer a healthy, but simple ecclesiology, because if our ecclesiology is bad, then our theology is probably bad also. If how we do church is trifling, unimportant, not a priority, or unmagnified, then our feeling toward God is trifling, unimportant, not a priority, and diminished. If church has become a closed-ended experience for us, then we probably have closed out the life-transforming power of God from the significant drama of our lives.

> **A healthy understanding of church is when church becomes the context where a God-centered life is integrated.**

A healthy understanding of church is when church becomes the context where a God-centered life is integrated. It is not closed-ended in a place, but it is an experience where all that we experience in God is manifested and demonstrated. Yes, it includes where we worship, but it's where we cultivate healthy relationships. It's where we get clear on our purpose in life as disciples of Jesus Christ. More significantly, it's the experience of where we get God's defining Word for our life. It's where our hearts are cultivated to become giving persons, persons who are willing to make sacrifice for some greater good. In the language of BMBC, the church is where we "GET It," an opportunity to Glorify God, Edify God's people, and Transform our community. It is an experience to participate in the unfolding of God's story.

Thus, when our appreciation of God is through the roof, we can't help but become the Church Through the Roof. Yet the sad and unfortunate truth of most churches and denominational agencies is that we are not through the roof because we are too content holding down the floor. Too many of our churches have reduced their witness to closed-ended stories reduced to rehearsals, reliving, and replaying old experiences. We have become content with doing what we have always done, with the same people we have always done it with, in the same ways that we have always done it. That's not Church Through the Roof. That's church holding down the floor. For too many of us, church is a place, a building, a structure, a business, or an institution. We will never be the Church Through the Roof when all we are doing is holding the floor down. When all we are doing is holding the floor down, we are also weighing down the church.

We are holding down the floor when we refuse vision. We are holding down the floor when we believe our best days were our past days. We are holding down the floor when we refuse to follow leadership into doing church in a new way. We are holding down the floor when no matter what the pastor envisions, we keep doing what we want to do. We are holding down the floor when we keep talking about the same old thing over and over again, and struggle to get one thing done so we can do something else.

How in the world can we go through the roof when a whole church can't even pay off two people? (This was a reference to an experience in the life of BMBC.) How in the world can we go through the roof when our doors are shut more hours in the week than they are open? How in the world can we go through the roof when we won't even show up to pray together, to study together, or learn how to be together? How can we be Church Through the Roof stuck in the same closed-ended stories?

We pastors have to examine our own stories sometimes. We have to be honest about our own faith journeys. I had to tell my people that I was not trying to leave and go anywhere. I would love to retire as the Pastor of BMBC, but I don't know how long I can pastor a church that seems content with just holding down the floor. A look into my journey raised questions about my own theological perspective. I have to examine what ministry in a closed-ended story says about me and my theology when the people I serve have a hold-the-floor-down ecclesiology.

How do we become Church Through the Roof? Let's consider the text. I believe the process of re-storying is in faithful interpretation of the biblical text. We don't have to make up anything or borrow from any other source. The Bible is replete with stories that are just waiting to become our story. I want to use the Mark 2 text to provide an overview of what I believe are three irreplaceable realities. After I provide an overview of the three irreplaceable realities, I will approach each one individually. Once I elucidate the three irreplaceable realities, I will provide a treatment of the seven dynamics that are essential to shaping the ministry story of Church Through the Roof.

Through this particular text, I assert that the re-storying of Church Through the Roof emphasizes and prioritizes that it is **all about Jesus.** The text says, *"And again He entered Capernaum, and it was heard that He was in the house."* The Message translation says it like this: "After a few days, Jesus returned to Capernaum, and word got around that he was back home." The church that goes through the roof is a church where Jesus is so central, it feels like Jesus's home. Jesus is at home in a church that goes through the roof. Church Through the Roof organizes around the story of the living presence of Jesus Christ. Church Through the Roof operates with a pervasive Christology, where the presence of Jesus is experienced in all the church says and does.

> The church that goes through the roof is a church where Jesus is so central, it feels like Jesus's home.

A popular text has Jesus say, *"Upon this rock, I will build my church."* The last time I checked, the word "my" indicated personal possession. The church is at its best when it is so possessed by Jesus that it feels like Jesus's home. Jesus should not be a stranger in His own home. Perhaps the reason we struggle at making guests feel at home in our churches is because we have even made Jesus feel like a stranger. Could it be that the reason our churches are just holding down the floor is because Jesus is not pervasive, but peripheral? He is so peripheral to what we do that He's a stranger in His own house. Don't tell me this can't happen! It happened in the Bible! Jesus entered the Temple one day and found it to be so strange that He got angry and started tearing up things and declared, *"My house shall be called a house of prayer and you have made it den of thieves."*

Perhaps the reason some of you feel like your church is being torn up is because it is! The old story of a tamed Jesus who never disturbs treasured traditions is being torn up. The old closed-end story of Jesus locked in yesterday is being torn up. Jesus is not Jesus of just yesterday, but He's the Jesus of yesterday, today, and forevermore. To reclaim His church, the Lord sometimes has to tear up some stuff to get it out of the hands of thieves. For too long, we have believed this is our church and have been stealing what doesn't belong to us. In the name of our treasured traditions, we've been guilty of stealing God's glory; stealing God's story; stealing God's authority; stealing God's attention; stealing God's tithes and offerings; stealing God's time; and stealing God's gifts!

I don't know about you, but I want to give the church back to Jesus. I want to give the Lord center stage! Give the Lord His glory! I want to give the Lord authority over my life and His church! I want to give the Lord my attention! I want to give the Lord His tithes, His offerings. I want to make sacrifices unto the Lord! I want to give the Lord reasonable service! I want to give the Lord honor, glory, and majesty. I want BMBC to be known as the church where the Lord lives!

The second irreplaceable reality that leaps from the text is where it is known that Jesus is in the house, **people are attracted.** *"Immediately many gathered together, so that there was no room to receive them."* Church became so full that the ushers couldn't find any seats for themselves. The people gathered together because they heard Jesus was in the house. The presence and power of Jesus attracted people to the church.

The church that goes through the roof attracts people. It has a welcoming and accepting anthropology. Like Jesus, it welcomes and accepts people regardless of their station in life. People who are attracted to Jesus are story people. Every person is living out a story, and stories are ways in which people connect. To overcome the ominous loneliness of our society, people are searching for connections, searching for common stories. Last year, I heard Bishop Love state something to the effect that "The first impression is the only impression."

I eat out a lot, and I know where the good food is in several cities. I can also tell you where the food is not good. I can tell you where the food is not good because I went there once! All it took was one bad experience, and there was no need for me to go back there anymore. So it is in the church! All it takes is one bad experience and our church loses its attraction. All it takes is one mean look, one cross word, one get-out-of-my-seat-I-sit-here-every-Sunday, one experience of being ignored, not seen, and not being helped. All it takes is for a person to hear you one time talking bad about your church, one time of talking bad about your pastor, or one time of disrespecting leadership. All it takes is one time for people to determine that a church does not represent their story and does not have any characters who would enhance their story.

> **We have created closed-ended stories based upon our personal comfort.**

As a pastor of thirty-one years, I have observed that in most churches, what really matters to its members is how comfortable the members feel. We have created closed-ended stories based upon our personal comfort. All we want out of our church is what we've been getting. I've witnessed it at BMBC. Too many of our people are only concerned about their personal comfort and not visitor attraction. We are literally stuck in closed-ended stories. We rush to the seat where we are comfortable. We sit next to who we are comfortable with. We only want to hear or see what makes us comfortable. We only do that which makes us comfortable. We only serve when we are comfortable, at the time when we are most comfortable, with the people we are most comfortable with. The conversation of the closed-ended church member is, "I ain't got time for that. I'm not going to do that. I've never done that before. I got something else to do. I can't work with her." We never look around and see who is visiting and how we might make our story more people attractive.

We have to work harder at becoming more attractive to other people versus trying to make the church comfortable for ourselves. Our story must be an inclusive story that attracts other people, inclusive of people who are different from us. Here is the litmus test of making the church attractive. Invite people! When making the church attractive becomes a priority, we invite people. We invite people because we know that their life story is similar to our life story. The reason why the house filled up in Capernaum was because people were invited.

When I visit these incredible ministries around the country, I always find someone to ask what makes that church great for them. The answer has strangely always been the same. People say that church is great for them because, "I feel welcomed and accepted." The people go out of their way to make the church attractive. No one ever says it is the preacher, the pastor, the deacons, or the trustees. I have never heard anyone say they joined because of the choir. That day is dead and gone! All I've ever heard was that the people at that church made other people feel welcomed and accepted. People connected their stories with other people. Maya Angelou once said, "People will forget what you say. They will forget what you do, but they will never forget how you made them feel."

Here is a powerful insight that I want to attach an assignment to: **Wherever Jesus is made to feel at home, it makes people feel at home!** When we welcome Him, we make others feel welcomed! I wish I could give every member of our church an assignment and they would do it. I would give the assignment to work harder at making our church attractive, and less on making ourselves comfortable. I would tell our people to invite people to church based upon the warmth they feel from him or her. Don't tell them about the pastor, the preaching, or the singing. Invite them based upon what they feel coming from you! Moreover, I would tell them to invite people who don't go to church.

(Please note again, it might take "some days." It will probably not happen overnight. It might take some days...)

Finally, the church that goes through the roof is **empowered by God's Word.** The text says, *"And He preached the Word to them."* The Word was being proclaimed in such a way that the church became so full, the only way more people were going to get in was by going through the roof. The Word was being so powerfully proclaimed, that church went through the roof.

> if ministry is not healing, it is not ministry, not even the preaching ministry.

I preached and taught this text before, and I believed that the Word referred exclusively to the Bible. I now acknowledge and confess that I was preaching a closed-ended hermeneutic. However, when I read what takes place in the next verses, I see something else. The activities in the next verses tell us that some people brought a man who was paralyzed. They brought a man who couldn't get to church or anywhere else without someone carrying him. They brought a man who was living out the narrative of broken story. As a responsible preacher and teacher, I have a practice of asking the text to explain itself. When I asked the text to explain to me what good a sermon was going to do for a paralyzed man, the answer I received was, "Nothing, unless..."

I've been around preaching all my life, and I have never seen a sermon do a paralyzed person any good—unless. What Mark wants us to see is that the Word Jesus preached was a healing Word. Preaching doesn't mean anything to anyone unless it's a healing word. My pastor, Dr. Johnny Ray Youngblood, has told me that if ministry is not healing, it is not ministry, not even the preaching ministry. Daniel Taylor says in *Tell Me A Story:*

> Individuals and whole societies struggle to live by stories that cannot sustain them. Stories that no longer provide the meaning and sense of purpose that life stories must provide are failed stories. If you cannot convincingly articulate a plot for your life, you are living a broken story.[12]

The church that goes through the roof is where the presence of Jesus so impacts the lives of people, the Word becomes a healing word. It takes a church where Jesus is central and the word is proclaimed to heal people who can't go anywhere unless someone brings them. There are people in all of our lives who are not going anywhere. They are paralyzed, unable to help themselves,

---

[12] Taylor, 3.

and they need a healing Word. People are healed when they are able to envision different outcomes in their life stories. People are healed when they are delivered from broken stories and connected to a life-giving story.

Our ministry is to honor God's Word to the degree that everything we do is empowered by the Word. At BMBC, we've been experimenting with small groups. Along with preaching and teaching, I believe small groups are the best way of carrying people into the presence of Jesus. We are seeking to use our small groups to allow people to experience the healing power of God's Word. It's within small groups where people can engage in the process of rewriting painful stories into joyful ones.

I had to tell my church that I apologize for not have any slick gimmicks. I was sorry that I didn't have any slick marketing tricks. I was sorry that I didn't have a silky marketing strategy. I had to tell them that all I have is God's Word. All I have is a commitment to a living story.

I now admonish every brother and I encourage every sister to get with a Word group! I pray that all in BMBC will get with some people who care about them. I want every member to get with a group where Jesus is central and the Word is being shared. I want our people to get with a group who is not trying to fix or rescue them, but is going to help them experience the healing power of God's Word.

I believe that when every member of our church becomes healed and empowered by God's Word, then church goes through the roof. Our ministry goes through the roof! Our outreach goes through the roof! Our Youth Ministry goes through the roof! The Brothers of Bethlehem go through the roof! The Sisters of Bethlehem go through the roof! Our worship goes through the worship! Our tithes and offerings go through the roof! I want Bethlehem to know that after seventy years, it's time to quit holding down the floor; let's become the church that goes through the roof!

QUESTIONS FOR GROUP DISCUSSION

1. Share some understanding of God that has shaped your concept of the church.

2. Identify an example of your church holding down the floor.

3. Think of some Bible story that can shape your church's story.

4. Thoughts on the three irreplaceable realities of Church Through the Roof.

5. What's in the way of you embracing these three irreplaceable realities?

3

JESUS IN THE HOUSE

TEXT: *"And again He entered Capernaum after some days, and it was heard that he was in the house." (Mark 2:1, NKJV)*

Several years ago, my youngest son, Ahkai, and I spent several days in Detroit. We had a lot of free time and ventured to the Ford Museum. There was a lot of stuff in the Ford Museum for us to see. We saw old refrigerators, old stoves, old televisions, and all types of household and technological gadgets from twentieth century America. There were all kinds of cars, every conceivable make and model. One item I will never forget is the actual bus that Rosa Parks rode on and refused to give up her seat. Ford had found the bus on eBay, bought it cheap, and restored it to its original state. We sat in the very seat where Rosa Parks sat while a video played to help us reimagine ourselves riding on the bus with her.

What struck me at the Ford Museum was this incredible display of household and technological gadgets, along with the Rosa Parks' bus, overshadowing what I thought should have been featured at the Ford Museum—Ford cars. We did sit in a Model A and Model T. We did view old Ford Galaxies and classic Mustangs, but the huge volume of other gadgets and motor vehicles from Motown's past eclipsed and diminished the one thing that made Ford Ford, which is Ford cars. I understand and appreciate the inclusion of all the other gadgets and other cars. It certainly made the museum interesting to have included all these relics from America's past, but isn't Ford Ford because of Ford automobiles?

I would visit the museum again and would encourage you to do likewise, but the Ford Museum represents an image of today's church. Today's church has a whole lot of things on display. We have worship props, instruments, and PA systems. We have stained glass windows, kitchens, and offices. We have state and national flags. We have beautifully framed pictures of the pastors, waterfalls, flat screen projectors, and until my life-sized image suffered a collapse, we had a life-sized image of me welcoming people to the Bethlehem Missionary Baptist Church. I believe our most treasured features are the finely dressed members who make their way to the sanctuary weekly to worship, to sing, to pray, and for fellowship. Yet, with all of our worship apparatus and ecclesiastical displays, have we not eclipsed and diminished the one thing that makes church church? All we do and have surely makes things interesting, but isn't church church because of Jesus? Shouldn't all we do serve to magnify Him in such a way that His presence, purpose, and power would be on display?

I have not always learned lessons and concepts immediately. I am the proverbial late bloomer in many things. As a seminarian at Vanderbilt, I did not immediately grasp the profundity of my amazing professors' thoughts. It was not until years later that I grasped the profundity of my theological professor, Sallie McFague. Sallie McFague viewed theology as metaphors. All thought and talk of God is cloaked in metaphors. Sallie told us that, "Metaphor is a way of knowing, not just a way of communicating. In metaphor, knowledge and its expression are one and the same." Karen Herring, the amazing tutor in spiritual writing, informs us that "Metaphors must be anchored in our experience and grounded in our rational understanding of it."[13]

> When it comes to the Christian faith, Jesus is the dominant metaphor.

When it comes to the Christian faith, Jesus is the dominant metaphor. The "I am" statements accredited to Jesus are undeniably metaphorical. What we know of Jesus is anchored in our experience and grounded in our rational understanding of Him. Thus, I'm rallied by this text, because everything about it centers around one thing: Jesus was in the house! This is a story that is shaped by one defining reality—Jesus was in the house. Everything that is experienced and understood is a response to one reality—Jesus was in the house.

The crowd came because Jesus was in the house. The place overflowed because Jesus was in the house. The word was preached because Jesus was in the house. Four able men brought one paralyzed man because Jesus was in the house. The four men were not discouraged to persist in spite of the impenetrable crowd because Jesus was in the house. They engaged in creative initiative and pursued a costly strategy by tearing up the roof because Jesus was in the house. A man was healed and commissioned to be a witness because Jesus was in the house.

---

[13] Herring, Karen, *Writing to Wake the Soul: Opening the Sacred Conversation Within*, (New York, NY: Atria Books, 2013), 16.

No one came there to see what people were wearing, how the choir was singing, or to hear the latest gossip. They came for one reason only—Jesus was in the house! The generous offering received that day was not given out of guilt or a sense of religious obligation. (It's not in the text, but I'm using my sanctified imagination to metaphorically suggest that people don't come into His presence without giving something.) They gave because Jesus was in the house. Even the enemy showed up, like anti-Obama Republicans, to discredit His initiatives to forgive and set free, for one reason only—Jesus was in the house.

Like Ford is known around the world for Fords, the church is known around the world for one thing and one thing only—Jesus. Perhaps we need to reimagine Jesus being present. Perhaps we need to re-story what we do by intentionally featuring Jesus. **When the church organizes all it does around the presence, teaching, and ministry of Jesus, we are on our way to becoming Church Through the Roof.** When the reality of Jesus becomes the defining characteristic of our church, crowds will come, the place will overflow, the word will be preached, people will start organizing to get people to come who normally wouldn't, some of our traditional structures will get torn up, the enemy will become more aggressive, but the good news is people will experience His forgiveness and will be healed from the paralyzing realities of their lives. With Jesus in the house, the broken, closed-ended, harmful stories will be dismantled and new wholesome, open, and healthy stories created. **Church Through the Roof is a natural response to one irreplaceable reality—Jesus in house!**

Please know that there is nothing we have; nothing we can give; nothing we can create, contrive, constitutionalize, revise, devise, or dramatize that can replace the importance of Jesus being in the house. We will live or we will die by our capacity to reimagine Jesus in the house. Our story becomes a viable story for new life because Jesus is in the house.

The late Thelma Osborn, a matriarch of our church, was a spiritual thermostat and thermometer of the Bethlehem Missionary Baptist Church. As a thermostat, she helped to set the spiritual temperature of the Bethlehem Missionary Baptist Church. When it was too cold, she helped to warm it up. As a spiritual thermometer, she monitored the spiritual atmosphere and would announce when the temperature was right by saying, "He's here!" When the spiritual climate was being unquestionably controlled by the spirit of the Lord Jesus, she would let the church know by shouting out, **"He's here!"** Her ecstatic proclamation provided spiritual narrative on the presence of Jesus. I want to set the claims of this chapter in Momma Osborn's proclamation and shape an acronym to explain the metaphorical reality of Jesus's presence. I want to use the word **HERE**. Grammatically speaking, "here" denotes presence. Through an acronym, I want to frame the presence of Jesus in the house by stating:

H – Hold the space,

E – Exhort the house,

R – Release the oppressed, and

E – Empower the paralyzed. It's all in the text.

The Bible says, *"Jesus was in the house."* He was not just in the house, He held a distinct and prominent space in the house. He wasn't stuck in some culturally biased picture as an empty symbol of some racist religious construct. He held the space of power and influence. The space He held was so noted, everyone in the house knew where He was, as well as those outside the house. Inside the house, they didn't have to look for Him. They knew where He was. From outside the house, verse 4 informs us that they *"uncovered the roof where He was."* His space was so prominent, people from outside the house could locate Him in the house.

Church Through the Roof must make certain that Jesus is holding the space. I learned this concept in psychology and counseling, but it carries over into the other venues of vital relationships. I learned that no matter how the counselee may act, react, transfer, or countertransfer, I needed to hold the space of a nonjudgmental, caring, and compassionate person. Even if they tell me they hate me, love me, or reveal something in their life that angers or disgusts me, I'm to hold the space. By holding the space, I provide an opportunity for a bad story to turn into a good story.

People in the house and outside the house will know that Jesus is in the house when His presence becomes so prominent, no matter what people may be experiencing in their lives, they will know He loves them unconditionally, cares about them in their situation, and is here for them no matter what. Even when our sins anger and disgust Him and our behavior makes us sick, Jesus holds the space because He is the *"Wonderful Counselor, Mighty God, Everlasting Father, Prince of Peace, Emmanuel, Redeemer, Lord of Lord, and King of Kings."*

The presence of Jesus should so dominate the story of church life that people will realize our problems do not matter. It doesn't matter your status in the church, or in the world. It doesn't matter how much money you have, or don't have. It doesn't matter how you are looked at in the world, or in the church, but when it comes to Church Through the Roof—He's holding the space! Just as the gates of hell shall not prevail against His church, no deluded, narcissistic, self-blinded preacher or leader can remove Him from His space. He holds the space as *"The image of the invisible God, first born over all creation…And He is before all things, and in Him all things consist. And He is the head of the body, the church, who is the beginning, the first born from the dead, that in all things He may have the preeminence."* The life of the church provides a story of hopeful transformation when Jesus holds the space.

> The presence of Jesus should so dominate the story of church life that people will realize our problems do not matter.

While holding the space of prominence and distinction, the Bible says, *"He preached the word to them."* In other words, He exhorted them. I have included a whole chapter on the matter of preaching a healing word, but suffice it to say that according to chapter 1, *"He taught them as having authority, and not as the scribes"* (1:22). He spoke with such power that unclean spirits and demonic thoughts had to flee. His teaching was such that all present began raising questions about their long treasured beliefs. His teaching was the impetus for new story lines in the lives of people. They asked, *"What is this? What new doctrine is this? He commands even the unclean spirits and they obey Him"* (1:27).

Church Through the Roof might hear my voice, but it hears His words. It is heard through my voice, or one of our minister's voices, but it's His words. We hear His words exhorting us, urging us, calling us to another level of living, loving, and serving. Like the indoctrinations of our slave experience, the people of Jesus's day had been given an oppressive world view. With the help of their own scribes, they were taught not to love themselves as God intended. They were forced to accept an oppressive world view. They were given a closed-ended story of the value of their lives. However, Jesus exhorted. He pulled that oppressive, stifling, crippling stuff out of them.

Church Through the Roof validates the presence of Jesus when we allow God to use us in exhortation. In the movie *Selma*, there is a church scene when Martin Luther King Jr. exhorts the people to fight for their rights. The FBI recorded the incident, and described Dr. King as inciting the people. J. Edgar Hoover's interpretation was not meant to uphold the strategy of King's exhortation, but in a very real sense, they were right. Exhortation does incite people to fight for what's right. Exhortation does incite people to live life as God intends. Exhortation does incite people to move beyond their small, selfish world and see God's big picture. Church Through the Roof sets the atmosphere where Jesus can exhort His people.

> Church Through the Roof doesn't just talk about Jesus, it allows Jesus to do what only Jesus can do.

Church Through the Roof doesn't just talk about Jesus, it allows Jesus to do what only Jesus can do. The one thing that Jesus can do is release people from oppressive powers and exploitative stories. **When Jesus is in the house, people are released from oppressive powers.** God's big picture always involves people being released from oppression. When the men lowered the paralytic into the presence of Jesus, the Bible says, ***"He said to the man, 'Son, your sins are forgiven you.'"***

I think one of the many mistakes of church history was the division of the Bible into the Old Testament and New Testament. By dividing the two books, we tend to place the New Testament over the Old, making the Old Testament less relevant than the New. We also make it look as if God was doing one thing in one Testament and something else in the other. The truth is what God was doing in the Old is the same as what He was doing in the New. The Bible is not two stories. It's one story that focuses on a loving God who is passionately concerned about setting people free to live out their God-intended story lines. God may have used different characters in different ways, but God was still doing what God was always doing—freeing people from oppressive powers. The story may have been in different settings, with different characters acting, but the plot and resolution were the same.

Read Exodus. God sent Moses to liberate the people from the oppressive powers of Egypt so they could serve Him. Oppressed people are incapable of serving God. Therefore, forgiveness is a political act where one who has power over another decides to set him or her free. Forgiveness always begins hierarchically, but ends up in relational equality. The strong forgive the weak. The wronged forgives the wrongdoer. The creditor forgives the debtor. God, the Creator, forgives us, the created.

> Jesus in the house is not a domesticated Jesus, but a sovereign presence in the house, impacting the world.

In our story, Jesus is in His place, and the paralyzed man is in his place. Jesus has the power. The man has no power. Jesus is experiencing value. The man is devalued. Jesus is living out His story of victorious love. The man is stuck in a story of victimization. Jesus forgives the man, thereby setting the man free to live in a restored relationship with God and his community. He was set free. He was released to live life unencumbered with guilt and shame.

Perhaps instead of Old Testament and New Testament, we need a Now Testament. Because then we would know that whenever Jesus is in the house, people can be set free. When Jesus is in the house, even the people outside the house can be released from what oppresses them. People need forgiveness now! Sin is oppressive now! Disobedience is oppressive now! Guilt is oppressive now! Shame is oppressive now! Pride can be oppressive now! Jesus frees us from that which oppresses us now! People can begin living out new stories of victorious living now!

Finally, when **Jesus is in the house, He empowers people to live life more fully.** When the scribes tried to diminish Jesus's place in the house, Jesus upped the ante. *"He said to the paralytic, 'I say to you, arise, take up your bed, and go to your house.'"* Jesus empowered the man to take His power and change his world. A man restored becomes a man re-storying.

Lest someone misses the point here and does what the American church has done, which is to make Jesus into a house slave, answering the beck and call of the overly indulged. Jesus in the house is not a domesticated Jesus, but a sovereign presence in the house, impacting the world. Just as the man left empowered, the people who gathered in the house were all going to leave, go back into their respective communities, and change their worlds. Like the man was told to go home, all of the people were going to have to return to their homes. However, when they returned, they were going to be different from how they had arrived. They were going to be different because they were going to be telling and living out a different story.

No one comes into the presence of Jesus and remains the same. We all come with some form of paralysis. All of us are not functioning at full capacity, but when Jesus holds the space, exhorts the house, releases us from our oppressions, we are empowered to change our world. The transformative power of Jesus restores us to re-story our world.

Not too many people ever heard of Ella Baker. There are no books written by Ella Baker. There were no great speeches given by Ella Baker. There were very few newspaper articles on Ella Baker, and no television interviews. However, as a member of the missionary in the black Baptist church, she was co-founder of SNNC. Some argue that Ella Baker made Jesus more real than Martin Luther King Jr. She was authentic grassroots. She spoke broken English that was rich in biblical story and prolific with indigenous metaphors. However, she was content being in the background, strategizing and empowering the people to act for themselves. It could be said that Ella Baker helped to make the movement a movement, whereas Martin Luther King Jr. was made by the movement. Ella Baker believed, like Jesus, that if the world is going to change, we need empowered people and not a powerful leader. Ella believed that if people saw themselves differently, they would live their lives differently.

Think about it! They crucified Jesus, but they didn't kill the movement. They placed him in a grave, but the movement lived on. They didn't kill the movement because God raised Him up and placed Jesus's spirit into His disciples. Jesus lived on because the story of His resurrection lives on. Story keeps a movement alive even when the author of the story is crucified and buried.

Church Through the Roof empowers people to join the Jesus movement and turn the world right side up. ***"Arise, take up your bed, and go to your house."*** Please know that you've been empowered to make this world a better place. You've been empowered to make Jesus real in the world. You've been empowered to let the world know that paralyzed people can walk! Paralyzed people can be whole! Paralyzed people can get up and change the world. People with broken stories can begin living healed stories, whole stories, and hopeful stories.

QUESTIONS FOR GROUP DISCUSSION

1. Name some of the prominent props in your church.

2. Where is Jesus in the life of your church?

3. Share a Jesus-based story of your life.

4. Provide an experience where your church can learn about the ministry and the witness of Ella Baker.

5. What's in the way of Jesus shaping the story of your life, your family, and your church?

4
ON BEING WELCOMING AND ACCEPTING

TEXT: *"And again He entered Capernaum after some days, and it was heard that He was in the house. Immediately many gathered together, so that there was no longer room to receive them, not even near the door. And He preached the word to them." (Mark 2:1–2, NKJV)*

"After a few days, Jesus returned to Capernaum, and word got around that he was back at home. A crowd gathered, jamming the entrance so no one could get in or out. He was teaching the Word." (Mark 2:1–2, The Message)

My childhood was marked by memorable trips to Louisiana. Louisiana is the home state of my parents. My parents would load us up in the car, and we would drive for two days to visit the warm and welcoming sites of their upbringing. We drove, sleeping in the car, only stopping for gas and the bathroom. It never dawned on me as a child that the reason we slept on the side of the road was because once we left California, blacks were not welcomed to sleep in hotels. Daddy never told us that the reason we were not going to the hotel was because we were black, so we would not be welcomed or accepted. Daddy knew I would ask, "Why?" Therefore, we had at least two extended stops in some dark rest area by the side of the road.

To make matters worse, once we arrived in the South, we were greeted with the Jim Crow signs of Whites Only and Colored Only. However, nothing about Jim Crow came close to the love I experienced through black Southern hospitality. I forgot all about the fact that during our long travels we didn't have access to hotels and were designated to certain water faucets and bathrooms, because the homes we visited went out of their way to make us feel welcomed and accepted. Being welcomed and accepted took away the pain of being unwelcomed and rejected.

When I consider the story of our text, it strikes me that this story is for a people who knew something about being unwelcomed and rejected. The people of Jesus's day were victimized by a Roman style Jim Crow. We all know that a part of the Jesus's story is that he was born in a manger because there was no room for his kind in the inn. The Jewish tax money was welcomed and accepted, but there were racist designations set aside for Jewish accommodations, with the Roman aristocrats having access to the best facilities. The segregation of the Jews was so ugly and intense that the Jews started segregating among one another, somewhat like what blacks did in "coloring," when we prefer light-skinned blacks over darker-skinned blacks. Jews likewise segregated,

> **What makes this story so incredibly important is that the presence of Jesus broke through the walls of racial, spiritual, and economic segregation.**

making some Jews feel unwelcomed and rejected. An expression of their religion mirrored their segregated culture with the Pharisees, literally known as "the separated ones." The Pharisees represented the religious sanctification of policies and practices making certain people feel unwelcomed and rejected.

What makes this story so incredibly important is that the presence of Jesus broke through the walls of racial, spiritual, and economic segregation. Like any good story, this story had a problem that would be challenged by the unfolding drama of the plot. The problem of exclusion was challenged so that the excluded would be included in this story. The text says, *"When word got around that he was back at home, a crowd gathered, jamming the entrance so no one could get in or out."* I don't know what kind of Jesus the white people had in Jim Crow South, but the Jesus of our text not only attracted crowds, he changed the crowd He attracted. It seems that Jesus made those He attracted attractive, because they became welcoming and accepting. It should be said that the presence of Jesus transforms crowds and make them welcoming and accepting. A high Christology creates a welcoming and accepting anthropology.

The story of our text provides testimony that Jesus attracts crowds. Whenever Jesus becomes the main attraction, crowds will come, and we do not have the power to self-determine who will be in the crowd. The catalyst for the Church Through the Roof experience is because Jesus attracts crowds! What takes church through the roof is the sense that all are welcomed and accepted by the One who is central to the gathering crowd. Once we begin functioning from a higher Christology, we automatically create space for a more inclusive anthropology. Moreover, we surrender our illusions of trying to control who has access to Jesus.

Consider the fact that the four men and the paralytic go to the roof because of the attractive dynamic of Jesus and the overflow crowd. There was a crowd because Jesus attracts all kinds of people. Again, note the issue of crowd control with Jesus is that we are not in control of the crowd He attracts, because He attracts all kinds of people. The crowds Jesus attracts are often in need of what they experienced in the presence of Jesus, which is to be welcomed and accepted. The church, the body of Christ, represents Jesus. We are representatives of Jesus when we do what He does, which is to welcome and accept everyone.

He doesn't just attract Jews, he attracts Gentiles. He just doesn't attract white people, he attracts black people. He doesn't just attract the healthy and well, with insurance cards, he attracts the sick and afflicted, even those without insurance cards. He doesn't just attract men, he attracts women. He doesn't attract just good people, he attracts bad people. He attracts the saint

> the population most clearly in need of feeling welcomed and accepted was the LGBT community.

and the sinner. He attracts the sweet smelling well dressed like Zacchaeus, and He attracts the smelly ragged like Simon the leper. He attracts men and women, girls and boys, and all in between. When I Googled the concept of being warm and accepting, the population most clearly in need of feeling welcomed and accepted was the LGBT community.

The Lesbian, Gay, Bisexual, and Transgender community has become the twenty-first century version of Matthew 25, when Jesus said, *"For I was hungry and you gave me food; I was thirsty and you gave me drink; I was a stranger and you took me in; I was naked and you clothed me; I was sick and you visited me; I was in prison and you came to Me. Inasmuch as you did it unto the least of these, you have done unto me."* I never thought I would ever have to tell the church, or even have the courage to tell the church, that the litmus test of Christian hospitality is in our treatment of the LGBT community. We cannot adulterate the gospel with our biases and bigotries, nor justify our intolerance, by being unwelcoming and rejecting. We dishonor Jesus when we cowardly couch homophobic amendments to our constitutions in response to a Supreme Court ruling that we don't fully understand. Jesus attracts all kinds of people, and He makes them feel welcomed and accepted.

I suspect nothing has more characterized life in America than the spirit of exclusion. The haughty arrogance of America, which deludes us into believing we are better than other folks, was created by the exclusive legacy of living in America. We have always found ways to reject and exclude people over something. From early childhood, we were propagandized into a narrative of exclusion, beginning with the sexes, evolving into the races, climaxing in classism, partisan politics, denominationalism, and now global triumphalism. We have found mean ways to reinforce a culture of rejection and exclusion, and we do so by theologizing our bigotries. Someone has aptly stated that we know we have made God in our image when God hates the same people we do.

As I pondered over how to unpack the meaning of being warm and accepting, the words of our text drew me in. It says, *"And again He entered Capernaum after some days, and it was heard that He was in the house. Immediately many gathered together..."* Two words caught my attention: Capernaum and "together." Capernaum was the place, or the city, and together describes how they gathered in that place. Capernaum literally means "village of Nahum," or "shelter of comfort," or "covering of compassion." It also means "covering of repentance," or where the mind is cleansed. "Together" in the Greek is *synago,* which means "gather" or "collect."

The gathering, or collecting, in the shelter of compassion, where the mind is cleansed, could be described as a shared space of compassionate service. In the presence of Jesus, our minds are cleansed of socially paralyzing beliefs and bigoted attitudes, and we come into a shared space of compassionate service. To the disciples' tendencies to set up hierarchies of exclusion, Jesus declared, *"For even the Son of Man came not to be served but to serve."*[14]

The tendency to set up hierarchies defined by power and control is always at the root of exclusion. "Our self-preoccupation and self-absorption are the root of the moral rot that we in the Christian West—and especially the United States—have been transporting globally in the name of freedom, democracy, private enterprise, and the good life."[15] The only way out of this downward moral spiral is through a gathering of shared space where minds are being

---

[14] Mark 10:45

[15] Carter Heyward, *Saving Jesus From Those Who Are Right: Rethinking What it means to be a Christian* (Minneapolis, MN: Fortress Press, 1999), xiii.

cleansed from socially paralyzing beliefs and bigoted attitudes and transformed into acts of service.

I want to unpack the issue of being welcoming and accepting using two words, one in an acronym and the other as a preface. I want to use the word "share" along with the acronym SERVE. I pray this isn't too convoluted, but it's all I've got. I believe these two words, "share" and SERVE, can be helpful in getting us to the place of truly being Church Through the Roof, because they facilitate the work of being welcoming and accepting.

I want to connect the word share with the acronym SERVE to say share space, share experiences, share relationships, share victories, and share excitement.

S – Space
E – Experience
R – Relationships
V – Victories
E – Excitement

It's all in the text. The Bible says they were gathered together. They were synago, in the same space. For them to get in the house and be together, they had to share space.

At Bethlehem, we've become intentional about the issue of sharing for the past year. It's even stated in our core values for group relationships (SEE APPENDIX). **We are a more welcoming and accepting people when we share space.** This means we are to provide a loving witness by our words, actions, and deeds that include all who are gathered. It's about being mindful that you don't take up all the room, do all the talking, all of the commenting, all of the suggesting, or even all of the praying. We share the space.

I've been in one-hour prayer meetings and witnessed one person praying for twenty minutes. If a room of twenty or thirty people gather for an hour and one person prays for twenty to thirty minutes, testifies for ten minutes, and sings for another ten, then that one person ends up eating up all the time from the other people. In a very real sense, we disempower other people when we take up all the space, and then we wonder why no one is in attendance.

I know no one wants to come and hear Bernstine do all the talking, do all the singing, do all the praying, and do all the preaching. As much as I believe

I have something of value to contribute, I don't want to hear me that much! I take away people's power when I hog up all the space with my words, my thoughts, my opinions, or my prayers.

The reason the people filled up the house was certainly because Jesus was there, but it was also because they welcomed and accepted others by sharing the space. The text tells us it was crowded! They knew that time was limited. Space was limited. Life was limited. And for everyone to truly experience Jesus, they had to share the space. There were other people who also needed to speak, others who also needed to sing, others who also needed to pray, and others who also needed to let the Lord know how grateful they were to be in His presence. I believe some of our most helpful and powerful testimonies are never heard because some of us hog up all the space. Let's welcome and accept others by being willing to share the space.

Because they shared the space, they all had opportunity to **share the experience.** All present were able to have an experience with the Lord, and all experienced Church Through the Roof. We make others more welcomed and accepted when we share the experience. Church Through the Roof wasn't just for the people who got there first, nor was it just for the paralyzed man. It was for all present.

As they gathered in shared space, all present heard the strange commotion as the men ascended the roof. All present saw the mud tiles breaking open, the palm tiled roof crumbling and falling down on the floor. I wouldn't be surprised if all present didn't get some dirt in their hair as the hole in the roof expanded. (Perhaps people will feel more welcomed and accepted if they got some of our church's mud in their hair or on their scalps.) All of them saw the strange scene as the man was lowered down, and all of them heard the heated exchange between Jesus and the scribes.

Earlier this year, we had the Reverend Jesse Jackson speak at BMBC. We had an overflowing crowd. People missed their own churches to be here, and some showed up who don't even attend church. Weeks later, I was still being stopped on the streets by people who were there. Why? Because they shared in the experience! They were there and all who were there will never be the same because we worked hard to make them feel welcomed into the experience.

Church Through the Roof is about sharing the experiences we have with the Lord. We have to make being here so exciting that we don't need a rock

> **The truth is no one can make us experience life like Jesus.**

star like Jesse Jackson, because for us, there is nobody like Jesus. We sing it all the time! "Can't nobody do me like Jesus!" What do you mean "do me like Jesus?" The truth is no one can make us experience life like Jesus. No one can make us feel so alive like Jesus! No can make us feel welcomed and accepted like Jesus! I don't know about you, but I mean it when I say, "Can't nobody do me like Jesus!" When we get real about our shared experiences with Jesus, we create the dynamic of Church Through the Roof.

I believe this next observation is a bit challenging for many of us. It's tough because American individualism has vexed us with an evil that has us claiming people as "my friends," "my wife," "my family," "my group," and even "my church." To truly be welcoming and accepting has to do with sharing relationships. The text says, *"Jesus was in the house and immediately many gathered together."* They were together. Together is one of the most defining characteristics of the New Testament church. The Bible mentions together nearly as much as it mentions love and three times more than it mentions money. Being together is a form of love, and love is always an expression of relationships. We make people welcomed and accepted when we share not only our common relationship with Jesus, but also our relationships with one another.

What makes church such a painful place for many people is that it can be lonely. We can be in the midst of a lot of people, but the lack of shared relationships makes it lonely. It's a sad fact that it's hard to break into a church community. We get up in our groups, our established relationships, and we struggle with including people. With all of this Jesus we claim to have, we make church a lonely place because of our inability or unwillingness to share relationships.

I've been called aloof and some other things because I know what it feels like to be alone. The truth is I truly want to be pastor to all the people, not just some people. However, one of the sociological and emotional nightmares of being a pastor is people being OK with sharing their pastor. It's a struggle because some of my members don't want to share me. I've been in conversations with new members and visitors when members just rudely break in as if no one is there. It's the James and John syndrome of church life. Jesus had the problem with James and John, who wanted to isolate Jesus and set up a Jesus-and-us society. Too many of us are just like James and John; we isolate and set up our own versions of Jesus-and-us societies.

However, to be a welcoming and accepting church, we must be willing to share relationships. I hold that the only way we are ever going to truly experience the love of God will be when we intentionally invite people into our circles of relationships. Don't you know that the more people you invite into your relationships, the more people you will have relationships with? We have to overcome the evil of American individualism, which makes us anti-relationships. Let's work on sharing relationships.

We are also welcoming and accepting when we share victories. Consider the text. All of the people were in the house, sharing space, sharing the experience and their relationships, when something unusual happens. A man, who they all knew was paralyzed, was suddenly healed and started walking. He hadn't been able to do anything for himself or for others, but now he had victory over his paralytic malady. The Bible says, *"All were amazed!"* All were astonished. All were impacted! In the language of my youth, "All were blown away!" The man being healed was through the roof! In other words, all in the house shared the victory of an encounter with Jesus.

> For us to be a welcoming and accepting church, we need to spend more time helping people cultivate joy in their own lives so they can celebrate with other people.

For some time, I've been bothered by the hate language in today's praise and preaching. I think preachers spend way too much time directing people's attention to who's hatin' on them rather than on who's loving them. The truth is there are haters. There are people who get no enjoyment when someone else gets blessed. However, I don't think we need to focus a lot of praise and preaching time on it. For us to be a welcoming and accepting church, we need to spend more time helping people cultivate joy in their own lives so they can celebrate with other people. Really, who wants to be around a lot of hatin' rhetoric? Who feels welcomed and accepted if all we are doing is putting people on red alert for haters?

The truth is, my brothers and sisters, when God blesses someone else, it's not just for them, it's for all of us. We give a different witness when we see what God is doing in someone else's life as being for all of our lives. This really rings true when God lifts someone up who's been down. Isn't that what resurrection faith is all about? It's about new life being given where death ought to be. We are Church Through the Roof when we share in the victories of those whom God gave new life. We become more welcoming and accepting when I see what God is doing for you as a testimony of what God can do for me.

When they shared the victory, the Bible says, *"All were amazed and glorified God, saying, 'We never saw anything like this before.'"* Finally, we **become a welcoming and accepting church when we share the excitement.** When we witness God doing a new thing in someone's life, our excitement makes it a new thing for all of us. Excitement is obvious. We can't hide excitement. Even if you have poker face, let God do something great in your life and it will show up in your expression.

> Racism has been a pervasive evil, invading and pervading all aspects of our humanity. One of those things is the distortion of our emotions.

Racism has done a lot of terrible things to black people. Racism has been a pervasive evil, invading and pervading all aspects of our humanity. One of those things is the distortion of our emotions. We show one thing when we really should be showing something else. We show madness more readily than gladness. We show anger more quickly than astonishment. We show despair more quickly than hopefulness. Racism, and its despair, has distorted our capacity to be truly excited. We distort our excitement by being ungrateful. Our lack of gratitude makes us unwelcoming and rejecting. It's impossible to be grateful and be unwelcoming and rejecting at the same time.

I'm reminded of another story in the Bible when Jesus healed a man and told him not to tell anyone. The Bible says the man did just the opposite. He went and spread it abroad. While we may critique the man and call him disobedient, Jesus never did. I believe God knows there are some things we can't keep to ourselves. When God has worked a mighty work in our lives, I don't believe God gets upset if we tell someone else. In fact, the worship of

God rises and falls on expressions of thanksgiving. The Bible says, ***"Enter into His gates with thanksgiving, and into His courts with praise."***

When we share the excitement, we welcome others to join in the excitement. We have a senior saint in our church who we call Mamma GG. Every time Mother Gloria "Mamma GG" Dawson gets up, she prefaces what she says with, "I'm excited." She can't even get to the podium and microphone without saying, "I'm excited!" As a child, Momma GG suffered from polio. Momma GG still has a severe and visible spinal disorder. Yet every time you see Momma GG, she's dressed sharp with a smile on her face, because Mamma GG knows what the Lord has done for her. Yes, she's excited!

I don't know about you, but I know what the Lord has done for me, and I'm so excited that if I had ten thousand tongues, I couldn't thank him enough. I'm so excited, I want all to know that what Jesus did for me, He can do for you. Share the excitement of Church Through the Roof! Share the excitement that the Lord is still setting people free! Share the excitement that someone else will know of God's love and acceptance.

QUESTIONS FOR GROUP DISCUSSION

1. How welcoming and accepting is your congregation?

2. Can your church pass the litmus test of welcoming and accepting the LGBT community? If not, why not?

3. How well does your church do in sharing relationships?

4. Discuss the author's meanings attached to the acronym SERVE.

5. What's in the way of your church becoming more welcoming and accepting?

5

PREACHING AND TEACHING A HEALING WORD

TEXT: *"And again He entered Capernaum after some days, and it was heard that He was in the house. Immediately many gathered together, so that there was no longer room to receive them, not even near the door. And he preached the word to them." (Mark 2:1–2, NKJV)*

> People basically come to church because they need help with something that's hurting them.

I am so moved by the focus of this chapter that I need to get right at it. I need to get right at it because it addresses two fundamental realities that I believe get lost in the way we do church. **The first has to do with why people come to church, and the second has to do with what they get when they come to church.**

Why do people come to church? People basically come to church because they need help with something that's hurting them. I know we say we come to praise the Lord, but behind the praise of the Lord is a person who's hurting from something. I know they look good, dressed up nice, hair fixed, makeup in place, and smiling, but behind the flair of the exterior is a person whose interior is hurting. I believe most of the violent and abusive behavior we are seeing in the world is because people are hurting! It is true, hurt people hurt other people.

As a part of the people who are identified as African Americans, I am acutely aware that we are not hurting from just one something. We are hurting from a lot of things. Like the people in our text, whose lives were being crushed by the empire of Roman oppression, black people are still being hurt simply by being black in America. Racism hurts. There is no painless way of doing or feeling racism. Racism is a hurtful ideology that continues to demonize America. It hurts when you are denied an opportunity on a job, in a class, or even in the marketplace just because you are black. It hurts when your loan application is not given the same considerations as another person, although your credit score is just as high. It hurts when your child is not given a chance to be the best he or she can be just because he or she is black. It hurts to see white politicians demean, demonize, and dehumanize the President of the United States just because he's black.

Poverty hurts. It hurts to not have access to adequate resources to live a life worthy of living. I know we come to church to praise the Lord, but we also bring the pain of living in cities where toxins have been dumped into the air, water polluted, and ground poisoned, causing disproportionate cases of asthma, cancer, multiple sclerosis, lupus, and other body system attacking aliments. It hurts to witness young black men and women give in to despair and turn their anger on one another, because they don't really believe black lives matter. It hurts when you are a woman and are not being paid or given the same opportunities as your male counterparts. It hurts when you get a certain age and it seems like you are being forgotten, looked over, and left out. It hurts when you are gay and people can't accept you just because you are someone different than they expect, based upon their understanding of gender identification. Mental illness hurts. It hurts when your mind gets sick and your behavior changes, and the people who should love you don't know how to love you.

> It hurts when you come to church and what you get at the church has nothing to do with what's hurting you.

You want to know something else that hurts? It hurts when you come to church and what you get at the church has nothing to do with what's hurting you. You come to our churches and all you hear is, "Praise the Lord!" "You ought to give God some praise!" "I don't know what you came to do, but I came to praise the Lord!" It hurts even more when the preacher stands and declares he has word from the Lord, but has nothing to say about what's hurting you, and more about what's hurting him. (I intentionally refer to male preachers because male preachers are doing most of the hurting by not allowing women to preach, who are usually more authentic about issues of hurting.) It hurts when the best the preacher has is a good-looking suit, an Internet sermon, some worn-out clichés, and an "ain't he all right" celebration.

Please understand that I know God is a good God, and God is worthy of our praise. Yet when I read the Bible and study our history, the people who praised God did so because they experienced a God who understood their hurt. The people praised God because they experienced a healing word in the midst of their hurt. In fact, their praise was real because they were real about their hurt.

I'm rallied by this text because it shows us why people came to church, and it also shows us what they got when they came to church. The text says that when they heard Jesus was in the house, they gathered. If chapter 2 is a continuation of the story from chapter 1, they came to church because Jesus healed, cast out oppressive spirits, and addressed the hurts of people. He didn't get up talking about church doctrine, why you are a Baptist, who should be in the pulpit, are why you should obey me because I'm the pastor. He didn't tell Bible stories without making them relevant to what was hurting the people. The very fact that people brought sick people to Him reveals that He was preaching a healing word.

> In his book *Jesus: A New Vision,* Marcus J. Borg writes:
> The synoptic gospels contain thirteen narratives of healings of particular conditions: fever, leprosy, paralysis, withered hand, bent back, hemorrhage, deafness and dumbness, blindness, dropsy, severed ear, and a sickness near death or paralysis.[16]

Recently, I raised a question with a group of preachers that I thought worthy of our answering. I wanted to know how much our preaching affects the ethos or the cultural characteristics of our congregations? I believe that what we preach and teach affects how the people behave, how they get along, their attitudes, and how they look at the world. Whatever Bethlehem is, it's because of what's been preached. If we are to be Church Through the Roof, we can't preach about stuff that holds people down. If we are going to be a hospital for sick souls, we can't preach and teach in hurtful ways, saying hurtful things. If we are to be Church Through the Roof, we need to be real about what's hurting us.

Please notice I don't say how we preach, I say what we preach! In the black church, there's more emphasis on how we preach than there is on what we preach. We are into the performance of preaching and not the purpose of

---

[16] Marcus J. Borg, *Jesus: A New Vision: Spirit, Culture, and the Life of Discipleship* (San Francisco, CA: Harper & Row, 1987), 65.

preaching. We have created what I call arena religion, where the value of our religious experience is on what we externally show rather than what we internally experience. We are more into emotional display than internal transformation. We say we had a good time if there was an emotional explosion and people acted out their pain in public display. We are into the external performance of faith rather than the inward transformation of faith. I see it all the time. Some folks never shout until they have done something on the program. We have done what Father Booth calls making a drug out of God,[17] where we equate having a good time in the Lord with how we feel rather than how much we have changed.

> We have created what I call arena religion, where the value of our religious experience is on what we externally show rather than what we internally experience.

The people heard that the "Word made flesh" was in the house. It was not the flesh made word. It was the healing power of God being manifested, embodied in the preaching of God's Word. How is a healing word proclaimed?

The first thing we note is that a healing word is compelling. It draws people. If the scene of the four men carrying the paralytic tells anything, it tells us that people will put forth extra effort to be in the presence of a healing word. People will put forth extra effort to get people to a word that will address that which is hurting them. People will get up early, drive extra miles, passing up hundreds of churches, just to get to some storefront to hear a word that heals.

In California, church life is being sabotaged by distractions and excuses. It doesn't take much for California Christians to get up on Sunday morning, get distracted, and find an excuse not to go to church. Yet when people know that the word will address what's hurting them, or hurting someone they know, they are more likely to stay focused and be compelled to put forth an extra effort. If you believe the preacher cares enough to shape a sermon with your

---

[17] Leo Booth, *When God Becomes a Drug: Understanding Religious Addiction & Religious Abuse* (SCP Limited, 1998).

hurt in mind, you will probably make a way to get to church and bring someone else. Some days, I pull up to Bethlehem and see cars everywhere, shiny cars. The lot is full and cars are on the streets. However, when I come inside, my spirit drops when I don't see a lot of people because most of the cars carried one person. A healing word ought to produce multiple occupancy vehicles. A healing word will put more cars in the commuter lane, because it compels people to put forth an extra effort to load the car up with passengers who need a word from the Lord.

The four men came and discovered the house was full and the entrance blocked. They couldn't get in though the normal avenues of entrance, so they went to the roof, and the Bible says, *"They uncovered the roof at the spot where Jesus was."* I don't believe I do exegetical injury to the text if I suggest that secondly, **a healing word exposes.** The uncovering of the roof can be symbolic of the fact that a healing word exposes some stuff. Again, too much of what we do in church and what we preach is externally motivated.

I had a classmate who could preach the horns off a billy goat, and he knew it. Before preaching, he would often brag, "Watch me shout that sister over there." When he hit his hum and started whooping, sure enough, that sister would be one of many who started shouting. A healing word does not preach for a shout, but for a change. We don't preach for effect, we preach for impact. We are not going to change from the outside in, but from the inside out. The stuff that's keeping us paralyzed is not external, it's inside us. Internalized oppression has paralyzed us to the degree that in the words of Carter G. Woodson in his book *The Mis-education of the Negro* says, "The white man no longer has to send us to the back door, we create back doors to go into."[18]

What's got us paralyzed is not outside of us, it's inside us and being released by acting out arena religion. What's got us paralyzed is in us and needs to be exposed. Think about it! Hatred is inside of us. Self-hatred is inside of us. Doubt is inside of us. Ignorance is inside of us. Jealousy and envy are inside of us. And all of that negative, self-defeating stuff needs to be exposed. Just pronounce the word "insecurity," and it suggests that what's

---

[18] Carter G. Woodson, *The Mis-Education of the Negro*, (Tribeca Books, US)

> A healing word exposes those oppressive realities that keep us bound, paralyzed, and not believing we have the capacity to change our destiny.

preventing us from living with a sense of confidence is inside of us. A healing word exposes those oppressive realities that keep us bound, paralyzed, and not believing we have the capacity to change our destiny.

The text tells us that when they let the man down, *"Jesus saw their faith."* Jesus saw the intentions of their actions in relationship to the man's condition. Faith is always intentional action in response to the human condition. **Thirdly, a healing word discloses.** A healing word sees faith in action.

Too much of our preaching is driven by our wanting to be seen. Preaching has been sabotaged by the third temptation, which is an insatiable desire for attention. Our desire to be seen preaching has become more important than what we say in our preaching. A healing word is a response to what is seen in the intent of faithful action. We have to look beyond the external appearances of people and see that people don't really come to church to see us preach. What's really got them there is some hurt, some painful issue, some problem that's in the way of wholesome living. Jesus said, *"I came that you might have life, and have it more abundantly."* We must preach because we see what's in the way of people living as God intends. Let's preach sermons based upon what faith discloses and love disposes.

Allow me to conclude by noting what Jesus does in response to faith in action. The Bible says, *"When Jesus saw their faith, He said to the paralytic, 'Son, your sins are forgiven.'"* Jesus saw the man's external condition, but responded to his internal condition. He saw what was being acted out, but He spoke to what was being carried within. The man was physically paralyzed because he was internally paralyzed. In the words of Howard Thurman, "Before we can ever experience transformation externally, we must be transformed internally."

Finally, a healing word disposes. Jesus's word of forgiveness was essentially a declaration of independence from internal oppression. Whatever was causing the man to be paralyzed physically, Jesus broke the chain by

> A healing word disposes of that which keeps people in bondage.

dealing with what held him paralyzed spiritually. A healing word disposes of that which keeps people in bondage. The people who come to our churches need to get rid of some stuff. The people who come to our churches have got some stuff on the inside that has them paralyzed on the outside. They need a word that will dispose of the external condition by disposing of the internal affliction. A lot of what our people act out is the result of what's happening within. That's why Jesus preached and healed, because there was healing in His preaching.

No wonder the Bible says, *"And the word became flesh and dwelt among us, and we beheld his glory as the only begotten of the Father."* In other words, He not only preached a healing word, but He lived and died a healing word. The Bible declares, *"Surely He has borne our griefs and carried our sorrows; yet we esteemed Him stricken, smitten by God, and afflicted. He was wounded for our transgressions. He was bruised for our iniquities. The chastisement of our peace was upon Him, and by his stripes we are healed."*

I don't know about you, but I was saved by a healing word. I was delivered by a healing word. I was redeemed by a healing word. And if I am to be all God ever wants me to be, it will because His word heals me. And when you see me shout, please know it's because, like the songwriter,

> He touched me,
> And made me whole

QUESTIONS FOR GROUP DISCUSSION

1. Why do you think people come to church?

2. Do you think people are getting from the church what they came for? Why?

3. Discuss how you feel when the church fails to address what's hurting you.

4. What was the topic of the last sermon you heard? And, what healing import did it carry?

5. If you are a preacher or teacher, what's in the way of you preaching or teaching a healing word?

6

COMPASSION

TEXT: *"And again He entered Capernaum after some days, and it was heard that He was in the house. Immediately many gathered together, so that there was no longer room to receive them, not even near the door. And He preached the word to them. Then they came to Him, bringing a paralytic who was carried by four men." (Mark 2:1–3, NKJV)*

Last year, a room full of scientists and astronomers jumped up and down, high-fived, and cried in jubilation as a space probe landed on a comet 310 million miles from the earth. The Rosetta mission launched ten years ago traveled 6.4 billion miles before making its historic rendezvous in August. The space probe is about the size of a washing machine and is now taking and transferring pictures back to earth, for what I don't know. I do know that whatever they are doing, it's the beginning of something else.

The great artist Pablo Picasso noted that, "Every child is an artist. The challenge is to remain an artist after you grow up." Jesus taught that, **"Unless we become as little children, we shall in no way enter the kingdom of God."** Paul said, **"Eye has not seen, ear has not heard, nor has it entered into the hearts of men, what great things which the Lord has prepared for those who love him."** John wrote, **"It has not yet appeared what we shall be, but it shall appear when we see Him as He is."**

The vision we are casting and carving about Church Through the Roof is an appeal to the creative potential in all of us. It is a summons to bring forth the artistic energy of the child and open our eyes, ears, and hearts to the great things the Lord has prepared. It is a call to embrace the not yet and to engage in the beginning of something else. I don't know about you, but I am thoroughly convinced that the words of our text represent God's Word for the local church, particularly BMBC, to begin living a life-giving story. Our story is to begin seeing ourselves as Church Through the Roof.

We are not changing what we are about. We will still offer what we know best - that Jesus saves to the utmost. We are still going to offer up what we do best - praise and worship to God's Holy Name. We are still going to offer up ourselves as sacrifices in Christian service, and we are going to remain loyal to our Baptist heritage. We are just changing the way we view ourselves and the way we talk about ourselves. Consequently, we want to be seen, engaged, and noted as a distinct and viable option for Christian community.

We have proposed three indispensable realities that, according to our text, uphold the narrative of Church Through the Roof. Those indispensable realties are:

1. **Jesus is in the house** – it's all about Him! Capernaum was his home! The Church Through the Roof has a sense in which Jesus is home. We aspire to a high Christology.
2. **Attractive to people** – it's a church where all people are made "welcomed and accepted." When the church makes Jesus feel at home, it makes people feel at home, no matter where they come from, their life situation, race, creed, or even sexual orientation. We aspire to an inclusive anthropology.
3. **A Healing Word** – must be preached. I like the way Dr. Mary Tolbert, my New Testament Professor at Vanderbilt, puts it, "A performative utterance." What Jesus says, happens; His word performs an act. It's not doctrinal buffoonery or moralistic superiority, but a word where the hurts of the world are healed by the grace of God. We aspire to a healing hermeneutic.

There are seven indispensable dynamics we noted in the text that are essential to the vision of Church Through the Roof. I want us to consider the first activity, which is dramatized in verse 3. I believe this one is first because without it, the others become, at best, mechanical, or at worst, crude. The first dynamic is compassion. Compassion is critical because it speaks of our innermost selves. In fact, the word used for compassion, "splangchna," refers to the entrails of the body, or as we put it in our community, the guts. Compassion is that which comes from our very center. We've heard people say, "I hate his guts." That's deep hatred, but we are referring to deep love. The Old Testament uses another word for compassion that refers to the womb of Yahweh. It is what God feels when God is about to birth a new beginning out of a painful reality.

Henri Nouwen tells of visiting Senator Hubert Humphrey to engage him in a conversation on compassion in politics. When asked about compassion, Senator Humphrey got up and grabbed a pencil. He pointed out the features of a pencil, the long stem with the lead running through it, and then he highlighted the eraser. He said the main part of the pencil was made to write, but the small rubber on the end is there to erase the mistakes the pencil makes. He said the main part of life is competition, and compassion erases the mistakes made out of life as a result of the competition. He said compassion is only called upon when things get out of hand.[19]

> "Compassion erases the mistakes made out of life as a result of the competition. He said compassion is only called upon when things get out of hand." Hubert Humphrey

We see in our text a snapshot of life, even church life. The text tells us that as soon as the word got out that Jesus was in the house, *"immediately many gathered together so that there was no longer room to receive them, not even near the door."* It reads like the people bum-rushed the place. People who don't think there's enough are always bum-rushing. It's about competition—to get mine before someone else gets mine and theirs. Like America, Rome was driven by the motivating energy of competition, not compassion. It was about who was going to be first; who can get ahead, who's going to make the most, create the best; who is going to be rewarded, distinguished, and come out on top. Like the stem of the pencil, competition is what drove the people, defined the people, and in so many ways, destroyed and isolated the people.

The cruel lead of competition is everywhere! Competition is what's distorting Washington. While politicians spend millions of dollars competing for seats, people are being beaten lower and lower into debt and despair. Economics and business have become such competitive forces that they brutalize people for profit. There is no excuse for the Ebola crisis other than the fact that pharmaceutical companies can, without conscience, watch black people die because there's no profit to be made from a poor black country. The irony is that African countries would not be poor if not for the thieving practices of white Europeans and Americans. I witness husbands and wives destroy loving relationships through competition. They argue over who's

---

[19] Henri J. M. Nouwen, Compassion: A Reflection on the Christian Life (New York, NY: Image Books by Doubleday, 1983), 5–6.

going to be right, who's going to come out on top, and such competition destroys relationships.

I attended Bishop College at the time when some of the brightest preaching minds and talents of the black church were there: Frederick D. Haynes III, Ralph D. West, Freddie Clark, the late Marvis P. May, Jeffery Johnson, and so many others. I've said on more than one occasion that I knew I was not the smartest person in the class, but I guarantee you no one worked harder. I've been driven by competition for so long that I have to work hard to turn it off. I know I'm not alone. We all are motivated by competition, and we need to start using the eraser of compassion to erase the pain caused by our competitive drives. Like the people in our text, competition is what drives us, defines us, and in so many ways isolates and destroys us.

In our text, four men decided they would use the eraser of compassion to get a man to Jesus. They made a conscious decision to offset the harm of competition with compassion. Apparently they, too, heard that Jesus was in the house. They, too, knew that when Jesus speaks, something happens. They saw the competitive crowd bum-rushing the house to get good seats. They even saw people rushing up front just to be nosy, curious, and judgmental. Like modern day Obama-hating Republicans, the scribes were there as obstructionists, trying do discredit Jesus, to eliminate him as a competitor for the loyalty of the people.

However, four compassionate brothers heard about Jesus and knew that Jesus was a man of compassion. They heard of his ministry to people who were hurt by competitiveness, and what they heard about him stirred up compassion in them. Perhaps they heard Him when He said, **"Be compassionate as your Father is compassionate."** I'm bothered by longtime church members who have heard so much about Jesus, yet it hasn't stirred up any Jesus in them. We have members who have been around Bethlehem for most of its seventy years who are still competing, wanting to be up front, always on the program, singing a song, in a position, and have something to say about everything. Some of them are so into competition based upon family history that they don't care who they hurt as long as they get what they want. In the Putnam disciple stage, it's living life from a childish perspective, almost infantile.[20]

---

[20] Jim Putnam, *Real-Life Discipleship Training Manual: Equipping Disciples Who Make Disciples* (Colorado Springs, CO: NavPress, 2010). This concept is discussed in this remarkable book on discipleship.

Yet, these four men prompted by the compassion of Jesus allowed them to use what they knew about Him to imitate Him. Look at the text! The text says, *"Then they came to Him, bringing a paralytic who was carried by four men."* Here it is, my sisters and brothers, compassion is movement. **Compassion mobilizes.** It stirs up something and gets us moving. People who are compassionate are people on the move.

> Whenever we start using the God within us to erase the hurts caused by competition, we start making a move toward where God is at work.

The text says they came to Him. Compassion is first and foremost a movement toward God. It is a movement toward where God is at work. Whenever we start using the God within us to erase the hurts caused by competition, we start making a move toward where God is at work.[21] God was at work in the house, so they made a movement to get where God was at work. The New Testament tells us that when Jesus saw the multitudes harassed and dejected like sheep without a shepherd, he was moved with compassion. When he saw the blind, the paralyzed, and the deaf being brought to him from all directions, he was moved with compassion. When he noticed the thousands who followed him hungry and tired, he was moved with compassion. When two blind men cried out to him, and the leper fell at his feet, and the widow of Nain was going to bury her son, He was moved with compassion. He tells a story about a man robbed and left for dead, but a Samaritan comes and is moved with compassion. If we take our lead from Jesus, Church Through the Roof is a compassionate move toward where God is at work.

May I also add that when we move toward where God is at work, we move away from our selfish, competitive nature. I'm hearing people talk a lot about a movement of God that basically satisfies their selfish, competitive nature. It's amazing how people shout and rejoice when we tell them God's getting ready to give them something. What about a movement toward God where God can use us to erase our competitive nature? If we are going to make a move toward

---

[21] Henry Blackaby, *Experiencing God: Knowing and Doing the Will of God* (Nashville, TN: B&H Publishing Group, 2008). In this transformative work, Blackaby points out that God is always at work, and that realizing where God is at work is pivotal to knowing and doing the will of God.

God, we do so by being compassionate. Let's move into God's presence with a heart that loves, with a soul that cares, and with the guts to do something different than what we've been doing. God is not impressed with all of our competitive movement to be bigger and better, number one, distinct, and on top of everything. God never honors the busyness of sacrifices when our hearts are far from Him. Compassion is a move toward where God is at work, and God is always at work.

The text says that, *"Then they were bringing a paralytic who was being carried by four men."* "Then" is an adverb signaling a specific point in time, which means at the time they heard Jesus was in the house, they made a move. They moved toward where God was at work, but not by themselves. **Compassion is also a movement with people God needs to work on.** They knew they couldn't heal the brother, so they took him to Who could.

The four men could have been like so many selfish church folk I hear talking about, "I'm going to get my blessing. I'm going to get my praise on. I'm going to get what's for me, because it is for me." But the four men knew, as we should know, that if God can do something for you, He can do for somebody else, and you and I can be the instruments to bring them so God can work on them. There are people in our homes, our community, and the world who need an experience with Jesus. There are more people in Richmond not going to church than there are going to church, and those people will only get to church if someone brings them.

Across the nation, a particular Sunday was designated as Bring a Young Black Man to Church Sunday. We should never have a hard time finding a young black man to bring to church. Yet we need to be mindful that young black men don't need a suit, a tie, or Stetson shoes. All they need is for us to love them enough to convince them that what we are doing for them is not about us, it's all about them. In so many ways, young black men are like the paralyzed man in our text; they lack the capacity of their own strength to get to Jesus. Let's be Church Through the Roof not because we are better than anybody, but because we love everybody.

The text says, *"Then they came to Him, bringing a paralytic who was carried by four men."* We move toward where God is at work. We move with people God needs to work on. And we also **move with people God can work**

with. Read further into the text. The text says, *"When Jesus saw their faith…"* God works with the faith of compassionate people, and those are the people we need to be moving with. Compassion is an expression of faith.

I recently visited South Africa and had opportunity to visit the Gandhi House. Mahatmas Gandhi was a trained Indian lawyer approaching life in three-piece suits. However, a painful and obviously racist and unjust experience among the oppressed in South Africa moved Gandhi to remove his three-piece suit and dedicate his life to compassionate engagement. He became a catalyst for moving people God could work with.

I had a crisis in belief once, and my late friend, Robert Stephens, told me I needed to give God something to work with. My situation was not about to change until I gave God something to work with. It didn't matter that I was a preacher, a pastor, or a so-called Christian, I had to give God something to work with. I've since learned that God gets the most out of my life when I work with other people who are giving God something to work with.

We become Church Through the Roof when compassion moves us to work with people God can work with. I've wasted a lot of pastoral years and increased my own frustration by trying to do ministry with people God can't work with. The reason God couldn't work with them was because they were unwilling to give God something to work with. In honest retrospect, I've retarded the progress of the church and caused BMBC harm by trying to work with people God can't work with. I know this is going to shake some of you, but God is not interested in nice people. God is not interested in people who have potential. God will never use someone who is trifling, disloyal, and undependable. If our text tells us anything, it tells us that God works with people who have faith.

> **Compassion is an exercise of faith.**

Compassion is an exercise of faith. It was not the faith of the paralyzed man, but it was the faith of the men who carried him. Faith fueled the compassion that moved the men. Faith organized the men, and faith persisted that they get the man to Jesus. The four men had faith to believe that if they could just get the paralyzed man to Jesus, everything would be all right.

I know you love your people, family, and friends. Keep loving them, but for the church to be Church Through the Roof, we must move forward with the people God can work with.

I read the other day that our failures will never stop God's future. I believe the man had a family, and he had a lot of nice people in his life, but God couldn't work with them. The man was never going to be healed with just family and nice people. The Lord worked with people who had faith. Faith looked at that man and decided he doesn't have to live like this for the rest of his life. Jim Putnam makes a powerful point when he notes that "You find out what a person values by how he (or she) treats people who can't add value to the person's reputation or success."[22]

So much for nice people. So much for people who just show up. For us to be Church Through the Roof, we need people God can work with. People God can work with are faithful in all things, especially those things that don't add value to their reputation or success. People God can work with are faithful in the little. People God can work with don't make excuses, they make arrangements. People God can work with show up and don't drop out. People God can work with are people who walk by faith and not by sight. People God can work with know that the battle is not ours, but is the Lord's. People God can work with know that with God, all things are possible. People God can work with trust in the Lord with all their hearts and lean not to their own understandings. People God can work with love God with all their hearts, all their minds, all their souls, and with all their strength. People God can work with say to God in word and deed:

> **Lord, I'm available to you, my will I give to you.**
> **I'll do what you say do, use me Lord.**
> **To show someone the way and enable me to say.**
> **My storage is empty, and I am available to you.**

---

[22] Jim Putnam, Church Is a Team Sport: *A Championship Strategy for Doing Ministry Together* (Grand Rapids, MI: Baker Books, 2008), 96.

QUESTIONS FOR GROUP DISCUSSION

1. How does compassion show up in your church's ministry?

2. Is compassion an obvious priority?

3. What are your thoughts on compassion as a response to our competitive drives and tendencies?

4. Discuss the "moves" articulated in the chapter.

5. What could get in the way of your church or ministry being compassionate?

7

COLLABORATION

TEXT: *"And again He entered Capernaum after some days, and it was heard He was in the house. Immediately many gathered together, so that there was no longer room to receive them, not even near the door. And he preached the word to them. Then they came to Him bringing a paralytic who was carried by four men. And when they could not come near Him because of the crowd, they uncovered the roof where He was. So when they had broken through, they let down the bed on which the paralytic was lying. When Jesus saw their faith, He said to the paralytic, 'Son, your sins are forgiven you.'" (Mark 2:1–5, NKJV)*

I want to open with a life-changing, church-changing thought that I didn't get from the church, but from Taco Bell. If this message helps you, thank God for Taco Bell. In a recent church workshop, a Taco Bell executive shared a video clip that noted Taco Bell works to be more about an experience. Taco Bell sells food, but promotes an experience. He further noted that the team members of Taco Bell must have the experience before they can give the experience.

> Church is really all about experiencing God.

Here it is: Church is really all about experiencing God. When it comes to our relationship with God and the Lord's church, people will only experience what we experience. Other people's experience with us will never exceed ours. It's impossible for people to get something we don't have to give. No wonder the psalmist said, ***"My soul makes its boast in the Lord and the humble hear it and be glad. Oh, magnify the Lord with me, and let us exalt His name together."***

It strikes me when I continue reading our text that the faithful, loving, compassionate, and collaborative work of these men was motivated by their own experience with Jesus. It's in the text. The text says, ***"And again He entered Capernaum…"*** In Chapter 1, verse 21, Jesus entered Capernaum and began a ministry that impacted the lives of a lot of people. Crazy church folk were healed (Mark 1:21–27), and a sick family member was restored to health and service (Mark 1:29–31). Moreover, the Bible says ***"He healed many who were sick with various disease and cast out demons,"*** and His teaching astonished them. My respect for biblical scholarship and my sanctified imagination allows me to imaginatively assert that these four men's lives were also impacted by their experience with Jesus when He entered Capernaum the first time. They had an experience with Jesus that they wanted to share; they wanted someone else to have the same experience they had.

The work of re-storying our ministry, or in the language of the market, branding our ministry as Church Through the Roof, we need to know that others will get only what we have. Church Through the Roof is about an experience where the people of God are impacted in life-changing ways. Again, Church Through the Roof is built upon the foundation that Jesus is in the house, people are attracted and made to feel welcomed and accepted, and a healing Word is preached. For others to have that experience, we have to be comfortable with the presence of Jesus in the house, so that others will be comfortable with Jesus. We have to feel welcomed and accepted before anyone else can feel welcomed and accepted. And before anyone else can be impacted by a healing Word, we have to have been impacted by a healing Word.

> Compassion is about looking into our own hearts, discovering what gives us pain, and refusing, under any circumstance whatsoever, to inflict that pain on anybody else.

I want to again emphasize that the primary activity of Church Through the Roof is compassion. Compassion is about looking into our own hearts, discovering what gives us pain, and refusing, under any circumstance whatsoever, to inflict that pain on anybody else. I shared in the previous chapter that compassion is what's needed to erase the pain and marginalization caused by domination competition. Compassion in our world is an unforgettable experience. These four men were moved by compassion to go where God was at work, to bring someone God needed to work on, and to go with others God could work with.

In this chapter, I want us to consider a second dynamic activity for Church Through the Roof: **collaboration.** The text tells us four men were carrying a paralyzed brother to Jesus. Jesus had so impacted their lives, as soon as they had an opportunity, they got together and made arrangements to carry someone who couldn't carry himself. They carried the man together. They lifted him on the roof together. And if any expenses were incurred, they shared in the expenses together. They tore up the roof together. They lowered him into the presence of Jesus together. And the Bible tells us that Jesus saw their faith, four men working together. They collaborated.

All of us are where we are because of some form of collaboration. We didn't get in the world by ourselves. No matter how our parents might presently feel about one another, at some point, they collaborated. Our birth was a collaborative effort by doctors and nurses, or by some country midwife. We might have grown up fast, but at some point in our childhood, someone carried us. We may have been weaned too soon and put down too early, but we were carried long enough until we figured out how to carry ourselves. Yet somewhere along the way, we lost the collaborative spirit, and we now find ourselves as people who are hard to work with.

The loss of collaboration is nowhere as evident as in the church. I watched my father for forty-plus years, and now my thirty-plus years, and have been astounded by the difficulty of collaboration in the church. In most churches, including BMBC, 20 percent of the people do 80 percent of the work, and 20 percent of the people give 80 percent of the money. I don't care how you look at it, there is nothing collaborative about a 20:80 ratio. The sad part about it is that we have normalized it. The normalization of the 20:80 ratio has produced the painful reality that the average church in America is failing.[23]

I don't know about you, but I know that me getting to Jesus was because some other people carried me. When I didn't have sense enough or resolve enough to carry myself, some loving people carried me in their prayers. Helen Keller once said, **"Alone we can do so little; together we can do so much."** Biblical wisdom admonishes, *"Two are better than one, because they have a good reward for their labor"* (Ecclesiastes 4:9).

The other week, I implored a few Brothers of Bethlehem to help me shape a Four-Man Ministry concept. I want to use this text to provide us four indispensable dynamics for a collaborative Men's Ministry. I asked men, but what the Lord has given me is not limited to men. For us to be Church Through the Roof, collaboration will be essential.

My late grandmother used to take rags and make the most wonderful quilts. To this day, I love quilts. I have a few quilts—all made from rags or

---

[23] Putnam, Church Is a Team Sport, 39.

leftover fabrics. (I was later informed that the leftover fabrics were referred to as "scraps.") How many of you know that your life would be tattered rags or scattered scraps if not for Jesus? Church Through the Roof is a beautiful quilt of rags. Therefore, I want to use **RAGS** as an acronym for us to shape what is evident in the text for collaboration. RAGS is our Church Through the Roof acronym for:

R – Relationships

A – Accountability

G – Goals

S – Sacrifice

The Christian faith is all about relationships. Every aspect of it, from giving to living, from worship to discipleship, is about relationships. It does not take a lot of imagination for us to see that the men who collaborated to carry the paralyzed man were in relationship. They knew one another, had spent some time with one another, and understood a few things about one another. Most of all, they knew the stories of one another and what a difference Jesus had made in each of their lives.

> Shared stories represent the fabric of relationships.

Collaboration involves being in relationship. To be in relationship, we have to spend time with one another, get to know one another, and share our stories. Shared stories represent the fabric of relationships. The other night, a sister introduced a guest preacher and declared that she knew her so well, she knew what she looked liked without her wig. In relationships, we have to be real. We have to take off our public presentations and let other people into our lives, especially our lives free of wigs. To be like Jesus, we have to be vulnerable and allow others to know us as we know each other.

What we are trying to do in our efforts to create and cultivate small groups is build genuine relationships. Our meeting on Sunday morning, all dressed up, wigged down, and weaved up, is essentially public presentation. In some ways, it's a show! To be in authentic relationship, we must move deeper than public presentation. We have to live deeper than show time level. We must use our core values as a tool for us to create and cultivate relationships where people can be real, authentic, vulnerable, and courageous. Help me, Taco Bell! That's the experience we must have before we can give it to anyone else. Jesus calls us into relationships where we can be real, vulnerable, and courageous with one another. Although such vulnerability might not be popular, the truth is, as Brene Brown puts it, "Vulnerability is the birthplace of love, belonging, joy, courage, empathy, and creativity."[24] If anyone is to ever get to Jesus through us, we are going to have create and cultivate experiences where people can get what everyone needs, and that's relationships.

Perhaps we need to rescue 1 Corinthians 13 from the wedding drama and place it where it belongs within Christian community. Church Through the Roof believes that "Love suffers long and is kind; love does not envy; does not parade itself, is not puffed up; does not seek its own, is not provoked, thinks no evil; does not rejoice in iniquity, but rejoices in the truth; bears all things, believes all things, hopes all things, endures all things. Love never fails."

Brene Brown helps us as well when she states, "We cultivate love when we allow our most vulnerable and powerful selves to be deeply seen and known, and when we honor the spiritual connection that grows from that offering with trust, respect, kindness, and affection."[25]

The second letter in our collaboration acronym stands for accountability. The four men who carried the paralytic to Jesus were in relationships that demanded accountability. In other words, they could count on each other to do their respective parts. Every man held up his corner. Every man was where he was supposed to be at the time he was supposed to be there, doing what he was supposed to do.

May I share a painful truth? I've never experienced that in the church. With all that people say God has done for them, why is it we can't depend on people to do anything for God? I believe the reason I've never seen accountability is because the church culture never demanded accountability. We make it too easy for people to be trifling and unaccountable. This is interesting, because the Bible says, "Each one of us will have to give account of himself to God." Somewhere I heard that people don't respond to what we expect, but to what we inspect.

---

[24] Brene Brown, *Daring Greatly: How the Courage to Be Vulnerable Transforms the Way We Live, Love, Parent, and Lead* (New York, NY: Gotham Books, 2012), 34.

[25] Ibid., 105.

Larry Osborne cites that the dynamics of a healthy team are teamwork, trust, and courage.[26] We re-story our congregations when we cultivate cultures that demand accountability. Church Through the Roof demands that we become more accountable. We have to do more calling people on their stuff. We don't have to be mean and unloving. We can lovingly ask people, "What are you doing? Can I count on you? Are you in?" I believe that's what the Brooklyn songwriter was getting at when he sang,

> **I need you**
> **You need me**
> **We're all a part of God's body**
> **Stand with me**
> **Agree with me**
> **We're all a part of God's body**
> **It is his will that every need be supplied**
> **You are important to me**
> **I need you to survive.**

The third letter of our acronym stands for **goal**. Look at the text. The text says that Jesus entered Capernaum. Jesus was in the house. They gathered to hear Him. Jesus preached the Word to them. The four men came to Him. When they could not get to Him, they uncovered the roof where He was. Everything they did had a single goal—get the man to Jesus. I've not yet read, nor heard, where the goal of the church has been changed. **The church exists for one primary goal—get people to Jesus.** We may all do different things, but the goal should be the same—get people to Jesus who would never get to Him on their own.

Collaboration happens when we have a common goal, and for BMBC, our goal is to get people in the best possible position for them to become a functioning disciple of Jesus Christ. We must constantly remind our people of our primary goal. Just tell them, "I know you are in the choir, but your goal is not to sing. It's to use the singing experience to put people into the best possible

---

[26] Larry W. Osborne, *The Unity Factor: Developing a Healthy Church Leadership Team* (Vista, CA: Owl's Nest Publishing, 1989), 52–60.

> As members of the Lord's church, all we do has but one goal - to get people in the best possible position to become functioning disciples of Jesus Christ.

position to become a functioning disciple of Jesus Christ. I know you are an usher, but your goal is not to just usher, but to use the dynamics of ushering to put people into the best possible position to become a functioning disciple of Jesus Christ. I know you are a trustee, or a deacon, but your goal is not just to take care of fiduciary responsibilities, or to support the pastor and care for the congregation, but to get people in position to become functioning disciples of Jesus Christ. Don't try to hide on me, young people! Our goal is not to entertain you or provide youth-related activities, but to get young people in the best possible position to become functioning disciples of Jesus Christ." As members of the Lord's church, all we do has but one goal—to get people in the best possible position to become functioning disciples of Jesus Christ.

Because of their common goal, when they could not get the man in one way, they didn't stop, complain, or turn on one another. Someone said, "The secret is to gang up on the problem, rather than on each other."

The four men working collaboratively reveal to us another essential for Church Through the Roof. They made **sacrifices.** Collaboration demands sacrifice. You might ask, "What sacrifice?" You might say, "I don't see any sacrifice." Look again! They collaborated in getting another brother to Jesus rather than running up in there as individuals. They sacrificed self-interest for the goal of the group. They sacrificed personal enrichment for the benefit of the community.

How many of us have attended an event and discovered there seems to always be room for one? That's the way most of us go at life, because there's always room for one. We are always looking out for number one—ourselves! Yet these brothers sacrificed self-interest for the goal of the group. They could have been like us, leave the brother or sister behind, and every man for him or herself. No wonder Paul said, *"Let each of you look out not only for his own interests, but also for the interests of others."*

The story is told of a mine worker in Ireland during the great potato famine of 1847. He brought his lunch to work each day, but he ate alone.

Stealing away from his coworkers, he would then open his lunch pail. The other workers burned with curiosity, wondering why he was hiding his lunch. They assumed he had some delicious morsels that he refused to share.

Finally, they could stand the suspense no longer. Someone opened his lunch pail to find it was full of potato peels. While his children were given the potatoes for their lunches, he took the peels. Isn't it ironic that his great sacrifice was actually assuring him he would get most of the vitamins and minerals that are contained in the potato? The most vitamins and minerals of a potato are in the peel. Not understanding what science has revealed to us in recent years, this father was enriching himself—rather than his children—with his sacrificial giving. That's what we do when we sacrifice, we end up enriching ourselves with a big heart, a creative mind, and a loving spirit.

That's something like what Jesus did. The Bible said, *"That being in the form of God, did not consider it robbery to be equal with God, but made himself of no reputation, taking the form of a bondservant, and coming in the likeness of man. And being found in the appearance of a man, He humbled Himself and became obedient to the point of death, even the death of the cross. Therefore God has also highly exalted Him and given Him the name which is above every name, that at the name of Jesus every knee shall bow and every tongue shall confess that Jesus Christ is Lord, to the glory of God the Father."*

Church Through the Roof happens when a few people collaborate to get someone to Jesus. Church Through the Roof happens when people who truly know Jesus want others to know Him as well. Jesus did not focus on self-interest. He sacrificed self-interest for you and for me.

QUESTIONS FOR GROUP DISCUSSION

1. What do you think about the idea of people experiencing the church we experience?

2. What has been your experience in church?

3. Describe an experience of authentic, selfless collaboration in your church.

4. Discuss the author's acronym: RAGS.

5. What gets in the way of your church living out RAGS?

8

CREATIVITY

TEXT: *"And again He entered Capernaum after some days, and it was heard that He was in the house. Immediately many gathered together, so that there was no longer room to receive them, not even near the door. And He preached the word to them. Then they came to Him, bringing a paralytic who was carried by four men. And when they could not come near Him because of the crowd, they uncovered the roof where He was. So when they had broken through, they let down the bed on which the paralytic was lying. When Jesus saw their faith, He said to the paralytic, 'Son, your sins are forgiven you.'"* (Mark 2:1–5, NKJV)

As I have sat with the text that guides and shapes these writings, I have been convicted on so many levels about how we do church. One of those convictions I want to explore and incorporate into this chapter. As long as we allow God to be God, God will reveal to us why God is God and not you or I. God has convicted me by allowing me to see that if I am not seeing people right, I probably am not seeing God right. If my perspective of people is skewed, twisted, and distorted, my perspective of God is most likely skewed, twisted, and distorted.

Jesus taught that if you come to the altar and discover you have sinned against a brother or sister, you ought to leave the altar and settle matters with your brother or sister, and then come back to the altar. Allow me a moment to leave the altar of my normal sermonic-shaped offerings and settle a matter with a brother who I have time and time again offended. I have offended this brother by doing to him what society does to marginalized people: we disempower them, and in some ways, dehumanize them. Ultimately, we take away their voices. The brooding outrage we are witnessing in our nation is the collective outrage of people whose voices have historically been ignored, because of their social location. The social locations of race, class, sex, or other isms basically put us on mute as it relates to justice and equality. Therefore, I want to submit to an offended

> The social locations of race, class, sex, or other isms basically put us on mute as it relates to justice and equality.

brother whose voice I have ignored because I failed to listen to him based upon his social location. I want to publically acknowledge my sin and plead for forgiveness and an opportunity to make amends.

The brother I refer to is the paralytic man in our text. Across the years, and even earlier in this book, I, along with so many preachers and teachers, have not allowed this man's voice to be heard. He's been in the story all the time, but I have failed to acknowledge the fact that the only reason he is in the story is because he wanted to be in the story. I have been blatant in ignoring the voice of a man who wanted to experience life like any other person, but I failed to hear him because he was paralyzed, on a pallet, and being carried by some other folks. With all of my sanctified claims of being saved, called to preach, sent to serve, with an anointing and the favor of God in my life, I have allowed who I am to not hear who he is. He's a man just like me. He's a human being just like me. Like all persons, he wanted to participate in life, as I have been privileged to do, and he even wants to do it with Jesus in his life.

I just provided you a living example of what this chapter is all about, which is creativity. Church Through the Roof understands the necessity for creative expressions of discipleship if we are to ever position people to do life with Jesus. Maya Angelou once stated, **"You can't use up creativity. The more you use, the more you have."** As long as I have been looking at this text, it never struck me that the man on the pallet had as much voice as the men carrying the pallet. In fact, he might have had more voice. If free will still means what it has always meant, then the paralyzed man had a voice in the decision and plan to get him to Jesus. I've not seen it in scripture, nor witnessed it in life, or ever heard about anyone being taken to Jesus screaming, kicking, and resisting. Jesus is a "whosoever will" Savior, not a whoever you make come to Him Savior.

Perhaps the death of creativity in the church is because we have subtly made church compulsory, rather than voluntary. It's hard to be lovingly creative when you are trying to make people do something. Leo Booth argues that the dominant theological construct of Western Christianity promotes an unhealthy relationship between God and people because it lacks creativity.[27]

---

[27] Leo Booth, *The Happy Heretic: Seven Spiritual Insights for Healing Religious Codependency* (Deerfield Beach, FL: Health Communications, Inc., 2012), 103–110.

Whenever our energies are used to force Jesus on someone, we dissipate our creative possibilities. The reason so many young adults leave church when they get to a certain age is because they were brutally forced at an earlier age. Church should be like the park: we take children to the park, but we don't force them to play. How much fun is forced play? Likewise, forced worship, and being forced to accept Jesus, is our way of admitting that we don't know how to make living for Jesus fun or creative.

So I thought we would give this paralyzed man on the pallet an opportunity to share his Church Through the Roof experience. If we listen to him, perhaps our own level of creativity will be heightened as we try to live out the dynamics of Church Through the Roof.

My youngest daughter, Kamilah, wears hearing aids. She has ears, and all the normal physical hearing organs, but she needs technological assistance to enhance what her physical organs cannot do. I want to provide a rhetorical hearing aid to help us hear the paralyzed brother on the pallet. The root word for being creative is create. Simply put, people who are creative create. I want to use the acronym **CREATE** to sensitize us to the creative dynamics of Church Through the Roof.

C – Collective willingness

R – Respectful group

E – Engaged in the process

A – Allowing new ideas to reshape challenges

T – Take risks

E – Expect God to be receptive

Again, the text says that when word got out Jesus was in the house, ***"Then they came to Him, bringing a paralytic who was carried by four men."*** The text tells us that four men were carrying one man. Historically, we have given all our attention to the four men, but basic mathematics tells me that $4 + 1 = 5$. There were five men in all, but the cruel hand of history has marginalized one of the men because he was paralyzed.

Notice the text says he was paralyzed. It does not say he was mute, so he could talk. It does not say he was comatose, so he was conscious. It does not say he was not dumb, so he could think. When the text identifies "they," it does not exclude the paralyzed man. I suspect that historically, we have read the man into the margins. Painfully, we read off the pages of significance human beings who are differently challenged. "They," however, included him. The text just notes that four were carrying him. The four men could not carry him if he didn't want to go, and God couldn't do anything for him if he wanted to stay just the way he was.

> Perhaps we would witness more people getting to Jesus if we softened our left-brain structures and included the people who are open for transformation in the process.

Left brain thinking stops on four, because four symbolizes structure, but the number five symbolizes the principles of multiplicity, progression, and passion and signifies the need for change, variety, and new growth. In metaphysics, the number five relates to personal freedom, making positive choices and major life changes, transformation and transmutation. Four represents structure, or a container. The four men represented the structure, or a container, but all five symbolized a choice to bring about a change. On the Fifth Day, the waters and the skies burst forth with an abundance of living creatures—a day of collective willingness.

Collective willingness is right brain thinking. It is the capacity to hear and include all people in a plan to make it better for all, which is a necessary dynamic of creativity. When the voice that is at risk of not being heard is heard, then great things can happen. The man on the pallet reveals that it took all five men to collectively will themselves to get the man to Jesus. Perhaps we would witness more people getting to Jesus if we softened our left brain structures and included the people who are open for transformation in the process.

We not only see collective willingness, but when we allow the paralyzed man's voice to get in the room, we also see a **respectful small group.** All five men were in, and all five men's voices were respected. Our work toward developing healthy small groups is a way of our experiencing Church Through the Roof. Jesus never did anything with crowds but teach and feed them. He never healed a crowd. He never anointed a crowd, or did like some preachers do today, "Declare and decree" some blessing on a crowd. Whenever Jesus changed someone's life, it was with small groups.

Moreover, the work Jesus wanted done in His name, He wanted done with small groups. Discipleship is not crowd work. It's the work of small groups. Most of the work Jesus did in preparing the disciples was to get them to work in respectful small groups. Perhaps it was the work of the small group that provided the space for this paralyzed brother's voice to be heard. People are more likely to come out of their self-imposed exiles and be vulnerable when they know their voice will be respected.

> Trying to do church with unengaged people is like a boy trying to play catch by himself, or a girl looking at a mirror that doesn't look back.

In the small group, they came to respect one another and knew they needed one another and could depend on one another. In a small group, intimacy is created and so is an opportunity for people to be truly known, loved, and respected for being whoever they are. I personally like the fact that the other four brothers didn't try to fix the paralyzed man. They left the fixing in the hands of the One who fixed them. I can testify that my most healing moments have not been in crowds, but in the respectful space of small groups.

A whole lot of creative energy is released in the space of respectful small groups. Let our church provide opportunity for respectful small groups, and we will witness Church Through the Roof. In respectful small groups, love will unleash a flood of creative energy, and all of us will be changed by the possibilities therein.

Consider the plurality of their creative adventure! The text says, *"They came to Him," "they could not come near," "they uncovered the roof," "they had broken through," "they let down the bed,"* and Jesus saw *"their faith."* "They" color this story. In other words, they were all **engaged.** Everybody was in! The man wanted to get to Jesus, and all five were engaged in getting the man to Jesus. **Creativity happens when all the people who can be affected by a process are engaged in the process.**

For too long, we have tried to do church with unengaged people. We've tried to bless unengaged people. Trying to do church with unengaged people is like a boy trying to play catch by himself, or a girl looking at a mirror that doesn't look back. In Acts, we see a portrait of a church creatively engaged.

They knew what Rome was doing to the people. They understood the realities of their oppression. This scene could have very well been a metaphor for Roman oppression. Like all oppressive constructs, Roman oppression was like trying to get in a house that didn't have room for everyone, not even at the door. Therefore, the people of God all became engaged in the process of making life livable for all the people in the process. As a result, they "were together and had all things in common."[28]

We have enough people in our congregation to change the lives of everyone connected to our congregation as well as thousands who are not. All it takes is for us all to get engaged and be creative enough to take the Church Through the Roof.

When the five men got to the house, they noted the crowd had blocked out access to Jesus. (Some people only come for the crowd, but these brothers came to see Jesus.) The normal means of getting to Jesus were not available. In the place of collective willingness, respectfulness, and engagement, they **allowed new ideas to reshape their challenge.** Another way of putting it is that they allowed room for looking at problems in healthy ways. They allowed room for ideas. Ideas are essentially looking at problems in healthy ways.

Getting in by the door or any normal way was out! Someone has aptly stated that, "Doors are for people with no imagination." Perhaps new ideas are so rare in the black Baptist church is because we are stuck on doors and lack imagination. I love Michael J. Fox's movie, Back to The Future. Some people get to the future by going backward. We have some people in our congregations who, if they had their way, would take us back to the future: the church of 1950, 1960, or 1970. It's hard for some of us to face the truth that the people who really need to see Jesus cannot get to Him through our so-called normal, denominational doors. The young black men, the single mothers with children, the aspiring young professionals with their families will only get to Jesus when we allow room for new ideas.

Let's not be so quick to shoot down a new idea. Creativity is in the business of birthing new ideas. Think about it! God sent us Jesus as a new idea. Jesus is God's new idea because the old one wasn't working. The church is supposed to be God's new idea, because the old idea wasn't working.

---

[28] Acts 2:44.

Out of their new idea, they decided to do something that had never been done before. They took to the roof! Please keep in mind you can't take a brother up on a roof if he doesn't want to go there. All five of the men

> "You never solve a problem on the level it was created."

decided to **take a risk** and go through the roof. I can just hear the brothers laughing as they start up the roof. Doing new things makes you laugh. Taking risks can be exhilarating. When we try something new, even our bodies become more alert and alive.

Someone has said, **"You never solve a problem on the level it was created."** If we have a problem on one level, let's go to the next level to solve it. If the door isn't working, let's go to the roof! If the normal ways of getting people to Jesus is not working, let's try something different. Let's go through the roof. The Bible says, *"When they had broken through…"* My Bapticostal leanings are pushing on me to acknowledge that taking risks requires a breakthrough. How many of you have had some doors shut in your face, but God gave you a breakthrough? How many of you have been turned back, discouraged, and didn't see your way, but God gave you a breakthrough? Someone needs to shout for the paralyzed man on the bed, because to get him to Jesus, they needed a breakthrough!

They got a breakthrough, and on the creative energy of collective willingness, respect, engagement, allowing for new ideas, and taking risks, **Jesus received them.** The Bible says, *"When Jesus saw their faith, He said to the paralytic, 'Son, your sins are forgiven.'"* I don't know what the man's sins were, just as he doesn't know what mine are. I do acknowledge my sin of not acknowledging him, but his sins are not mentioned in the text. But whatever his sins were, the Lord Jesus loved and accepted him. Forgiveness is the primary act of love. Paul Ferrini stated, "That whatever is not loving must be forgiven."

No wonder the Bible says, *"All have sinned and come short of the glory of God,"* because all of us have done some things, said some things, or thought some things that were not loving. Some of us have looked at people in ways that did not demonstrate love. Some of you good Christians have taught some things, preached some things, and believed some things that were not loving. Most of the preaching currently responding to same-sex marriages is as unloving as whites once were to black equality. The good news of the text is that love is the most creative force in the universe, and if we do all in our power to get to Jesus, God will do all in His power to forgive us. God's love is so creative that God will go through the roof to forgive us.

Church Through the Roof is a witness to God's creative love. God loved us so much, He showed up among the marginalized. He spoke up for the voiceless. He went up to the powerful to stand up for the disempowered. He loved up the loveless and prayed up the helpless. He was lifted up among riotous rebels, and He was lowered down in a borrowed tomb. Yet God raised Him up and gave Him power to create a new me and a new you.

God's love is so creative, God has promised a new heaven and a new earth. A new earth where justice rolls down like water and righteousness is like a mighty stream. A new earth where Trayvon Martins and Michael Browns don't die and where George Zimmermans and Darren Wilsons don't get away. A new earth where mother's tears are wiped away and fathers study war no more. A new earth where sheep lay down with lions and instruments of destruction are converted into tools of production. A new earth where the weary are at rest.

QUESTIONS FOR GROUP DISCUSSION

1. Discuss the author's acknowledgment of marginalizing the man on the pallet.

2. Can you name some other people in the Bible who have been marginalized by traditional biblical interpretation?

3. How does the lack of creativity inhibit our capacity to love?

4. Discuss how a lack of creativity inhibits the church from reaching certain people.

5. What are your reactions to the author's acronym CREATE?

6. What is in the way of your church being more creative?

9
CONFLICT

TEXT: *"And when some of the scribes were sitting there and reasoning in their hearts, 'Why does this Man speak blasphemies like this? Who can forgive sins but God alone?' But immediately, when Jesus perceived in His spirit that they reasoned thus within themselves, He said to them, 'Why do you reason about these things in your hearts? Which is easier to say to the paralytic, "Your sins are forgiven you," or to say, "Arise, take up your bed and walk?" But that you may know that the Son of Man has power on earth to forgive sins'—He said to the paralytic, 'I say to you, arise, take up your bed and go to your house.'" (Mark 2:6–11, NKJV)*

There are some things in life we will never live without, while at the same time being something we don't ever enjoy living with. This chapter deals with the one thing we will never live without while at the same time we don't ever want to live with. Conflict is the one thing we will always have in our lives, and be the one thing we least enjoy living with. In fact, many Christians assume that there is something unchristian about conflict. The truth is, just as there is no living without conflict, there is no Christianity without conflict. Christianity is a conflict-ridden faith.

Consider that in most Christian churches, at least once a month, we are invited to a table that was set in conflict. The Lord's Supper is set in conflict. It reads, **"On the night in which He was betrayed, He took bread and broke it. Saying, 'This is my body which is broken for you.'"** Conflict! Paul noted that at the core of our lives is an eternal conflict. **"For the good that I will to do, I do not do; but the evil I will not to do, that I practice."** Paul noted that we have a war going on within us. It is safe to say that the reason the New Testament was written and canonized into twenty-seven books is because of church conflict. Most of the books in the New Testament were written because Christianity is a conflict-ridden faith.

If we paid any attention to our world in recent days, we know that our world is rife with conflict. We have conflict from ISIS in the Middle East to the growing uproars in our cities across the nation. Conflicts are real from the White House, church house, your house, and with the people who have no house. Here at the Lord's table, in our times, in our lives, and even in our text, there is the reality of conflict. In fact, some scholars have identified this portion of Mark as being the beginning of a series of conflict stories. Thus, we have conflict in our times, at the table, and in our text.

In the previous chapter, I opened by noting that as long as we allow God to be God, God will show us why God is God and not you or I. Such awareness opened up for me to see that if we are not viewing people right, we are probably not viewing God right. If our perspective of people is skewed, twisted, and distorted, our perspective of God is probably skewed, twisted, and distorted. I openly confessed that I had allowed a skewed, twisted, and distorted perception of the paralyzed man in the text to push him into the margins. I hermeneutically hushed his voice, and in a profound way, blinded myself to the creative power of God's intervention in Jesus Christ. I focused my attention on the four men carrying the pallet and failed to see the brother as a willing participant in his own healing and deliverance. God helped me see beyond the structured four to the creative five.

> Whenever people collaboratively and creatively get to Jesus, Jesus will change that situation.

The Lord has shown me something else I want you to see with me. I need you to see that not only when we are not viewing people right, we are probably not viewing God right. I also see that when we don't view God right, we are probably not viewing people right. Just as bad anthropology makes for bad theology, bad theology makes for bad anthropology. Herein is the conflict of our text. The conflict in our text not only exposes the reality of marginalized people, but it also reveals the reality of a marginalized God. God gets marginalized in a ghetto of religious assumptions.

The five-man team collaborated, and creatively got to Jesus, but once Jesus did what He always does, it stirred up a conflict. Whenever people collaboratively and creatively get to Jesus, Jesus will change that situation. Changing situations and circumstances are inevitable contexts for conflict. The text tells us that, *"When Jesus saw their faith, He said to the paralytic, 'Son, your sins are forgiven you.' And some of the scribes were sitting there and reasoning in their hearts. Why does this Man speak blasphemies? Who can forgive sins but God alone?"*

There was Jesus joining with God in God's work, which is to make the love of God real in the world by accepting people whoever they are, loving them unconditionally, and forgiving them, and the scribes felt insulted. They, in essence, marginalized God to the belief system that they controlled. They limited God to the margins of their religious assumptions. Since the scribes were the guardians of how Judaism was practiced, the scribes believed anyone who does anything that has something to do with God must come through them. They did not care that this man's condition hindered him from being an active participant in society. They didn't care that he wanted to do something different with his life. The only thing they cared about was the belief system they controlled, and Jesus was violating it by speaking words of forgiveness without their approval.

Notice the scribes stated that the conflict was over the issue of how could this man do what only God can do? They saw a man and not God. Their anthropology distorted their theology, and vice versa. They failed to see that anyone who loves unconditionally, accepts people regardless of who they are, and offers forgiveness makes God real in the world. The reason why our world is so filled with conflict is because God has been marginalized, pushed into the margins of ghettoized religiosity. We are too busy looking at the humanity of people and can't see the divinity of God. We strangely limit God by not doing what each one of us can do, which is to embody unconditional love, acceptance, and forgiveness. Stevie Wonder was right when he sang, "Love is in need of love, today."

> If God wasn't so marginalized by the church, we could deal with the conflicts of our world in healthy ways.

If God wasn't so marginalized by the church, we could deal with the conflicts of our world in healthy ways. God is marginalized when we limit love to church talk and church songs and not in our day-to-day lives. God is marginalized when a religion feels justified in televising the chopping off of men's heads to make some senseless point, or to receive some fantasized heavenly reward. God is marginalized when justice becomes blind to the long history of racial injustice. God is marginalized when rich church people believe God has favored them and not the poor. God is marginalized when a Christian woman steps up to the microphone and says, "First giving honor to God" and then says, "I'm not going to forgive the police for choking my son."

We have an opportunity to learn that Church Through the Roof provides a witness where conflict is dealt with in healthy ways. Since conflict is inevitable, since conflict is a part of our human existence, since conflict is built into the Christian faith, since conflict will meet us every time we come to the table or the text, we might as well consult with Jesus on how to deal with conflict in healthy ways.

If we do not deal with conflict in healthy ways, we condemn ourselves to the bestial activities of a church holding down the floor, with members who are only concerned with standing their ground. Conflict need not destroy anyone, and certainly should not destroy a local church or a national convention. Jesus said, **"Upon this rock I will build my church and the gates of hell shall not prevail against it."**

I want to provide another acronym that hopefully helps us to hear this text and prepare us to deal with conflict in healthy ways. I want to use the word HEALTH to unpack this text and package this lesson. I see in this text some helpful and healthy hints on how to deal with conflict. Church Through the Roof deals with conflict by

H – Handle it quickly
E – Explore the emotional attachment
A – Assess the spiritual/theological issue
L – Locate a point of agreement
T – Teaching moment
H – Help someone in the process

The text tells us that when the scribes began reasoning in their hearts, **"'Why does this Man speaks blasphemies like this? Who can forgive sins but God alone?' But immediately, when Jesus perceived in His spirit that they reasoned thus within themselves, He said to them…"** In other words, as soon as Jesus was able to discern that there was a conflicting spirit, He immediately moved to handle it.

If we are to be Church Through the Roof, we must handle conflict quickly. Someone noted, and I quote, that "The only kind of bad conflict is unresolved conflict." Unresolved conflicts are those things we let linger and fester and become poisonous and cancerous. I've seen it in church, family, life, and even within myself that we have a tendency to not deal with conflicts when they arise. We let stuff stack up, and when stuff stacks up, it builds up, and one day, it blows up.

It's amazing how one conflict left unresolved becomes the power source for a massive explosion. What we are seeing in America is not Ferguson,

Missouri or Staten Island, New York. What we are experiencing in America is the unresolved conflict of how the voices of marginalized people have been historically ignored when faced with obvious injustices. Police have been killing black men for a long time. Women have been abused for a long time. Children have been abused for a long time. Racism has vexed America for a long time.

Let's learn from Jesus, and whenever we discern a conflict, let's handle it quickly. As soon as we sense that someone is in disagreement, let's deal with it. Conflict cannot survive without our participation. Let's not get on the phone and seek allies. Let's not politicize and use conflict to advance an agenda. Let's not demonize those who disagree with us. Let's go to our brother or our sister and handle it quickly.

> We have to honor what people believe, even if it's wrong.

The text tells us the scribes reasoned in their hearts. We are also told Jesus discerned that they reasoned within themselves. The reasoning in their hearts revealed that they had some strong emotional attachment to how they felt about what Jesus did. They were not just slightly miffed; they were appalled. It bothered them deeply because they had strong emotional attachment to what they believed about people and God.

Conflict is dealt with in healthy ways when we explore people's emotional attachment to their disagreements. The scribes help us see that when it comes to religion, people have strong emotional attachments. I'm still learning as a pastor that I might believe myself right in doing certain things, but I need to honor people's emotional attachments. We can't change people's emotional attachments by disrupting their world. We have to honor what people believe, even if it's wrong. None of us are possessors of absolute truth. The truth is all of us know only in part. We all are seeing through the glass dimly. We show people we love them even when we disagree with them when we honor what they are emotionally attached to.

Jesus honored their emotional attachment, and then He assessed for spiritual or theological value. He heard what they said, *"How can this man do what only God can do?"* Although they were emotionally attached to what they believed, Jesus wanted to be sure He understood what they believed. Stephen Covey stated in his book, *The 7 Habits of Highly Effective People,* that if you want to be understood, seek to understand. Jesus understood that the theological issue was acts of man versus acts of God. Can human beings do what they believed only God could do? For believers, and even sometimes for nonbelievers, **conflict is dealt with in healthy ways when we can assess the theological/spiritual issue.**

We are better prepared to handle conflict in healthy ways when we can hear beyond the emotions and into the belief system. It's helpful to all parties concerned when we understand the God issue. What has this conflict to do with God? What is this conflict revealing about what this person believes about God, as well as about human beings? We get a sense of what most needs to be addressed when we assess the God issue. In most conflicts among church folk, the God issue will decide what needs to take place to get to a resolution. Unfortunately, we have to be on guard for the Evil One, because some folks don't care what God has to say. Some folks just want their way, because in their infantile state of existence, they are god. Some folks have an idolized image of themselves as their god-construct. It has been wisely stated, "You know that you have made God in your own image when God dislikes the same people you do."

Jesus assessed the theological issue and then **moved to locate a point of agreement.** He didn't beat them down with a persuasive argument. He didn't force His opinion upon them. He just used what He knew about them to invite them to consider their untenable position. He asked, *"Which is easier to say to the paralytic, 'Your sins are forgiven you,' or to say, 'Arise, take up your bed and walk?'"* We deal with conflict in healthy ways when we can **locate points of agreement.** We experience a shift in the process when we can move from hard disagreements to soft agreements.

There was no disagreement that the man was paralyzed. There was no disagreement that his paralysis prevented him from participating in life as a healthy, wholesome, and productive person. Both Jesus and the scribes agreed that something can be said about forgiveness and something can be said about getting up and walking. Where they disagreed was on Who needs to say it.

One of the common points of contention in relationships is not what needs to be done, but who needs to authorize it being done. Church conflicts are often rooted in not on what needs to be done, but who needs to authorize it. My places of pastoral conflicts have never been on what needs to be done. Everybody agrees it needs to be done! The points of disagreement have always been on who needs to authorize it.

Our challenge is always to get us to the places where we agree and then we might agree on who needs to authorize it. Jesus located the place of agreement and then proceeded to use it as a teaching moment. He says in verse 10, *"'That you may know that the Son of Man has power on earth to forgive sins'"— He said to the paralytic, "'I say to you, arise, take up our bed, and go to your house.'"* We deal with conflict in healthy ways when we can use it as a **teaching moment.** Since we are going to experience conflict, let's learn something from it.

I really don't want you to miss this. He says, *"That you may know..."* Their conflict was in their understanding of what they thought they knew about God, sin, and human beings. Their point of conflict was on what they believed about acts of God and acts of human beings. Jesus used this as a teaching moment by not pointing out God. He does not say, **Son of God.** He used the Ezekiel term, **Son of Man,** which means son of the human experience. Since they all agreed that perhaps speaking words of forgiveness, even from the perspective of God, is much easier than speaking words of resurrection, or words of new life, Jesus proceeded to speak of them both from the perspective of the human experience. He spoke of forgiveness and new life from the perspective of the human experience. What mattered the most was what forgiveness as well as new life have to do with the human experience.

In places of conflict, we do well to use them as teaching moments where we do what we know God wants done, which is to speak words of forgiveness and new life. Please know that **there is no place of conflict where forgiveness will not infuse it with new life.** There is no one we are in conflict with who can't learn something about God through us when we speak words of forgiveness and new life. In fact, the reality of forgiveness will bring forth new life. Since we are all sons and daughters of the human experience, we know that all within the human experience need forgiveness for something. We need not stay paralyzed in places of conflict, let's use conflict as teaching moments where the very power of God can show up in a human experience and infuse it with forgiveness and new life. Being truly forgiven is to experience new life!

Jesus also used conflict as an opportunity to **help someone.** He said to the paralytic, *"I say to you, arise, take up your bed and go to your house."* Jesus used an experience of conflict to help a brother be a better brother. He used it to help a man be a better man. He used it to help a family man be a better family man. He used conflict to make a human being a better human being,

> Healthy conflicts helps people. Healthy conflict doesn't leave people paralyzed in pain and insensitivity.

which would make his community a better community.

Healthy conflicts helps people. Healthy conflict doesn't leave people paralyzed in pain and insensitivity. Since we are going to have conflict in our lives, conflict in our selves, conflict in relationships, conflict in the world, and conflict in the church, let's use it to help someone. In other words, don't waste conflict experiences. Use what you're going through to help someone else. We all know that it takes hot water to make tea. It takes a squeezed lemon to make lemonade. It takes smashing grapes to get wine. It takes a hot iron to smooth wrinkles and a hot oven to bake a cake. It takes agitation to break free the dirt and grime. It takes scrubbing to get a shine. It took a crucified Savior to save you and to save me.

Jesus did not waste conflict. Jesus did not waste what He went through. He used the conflict of disagreement, disrespect, disowning, and desertion for salvific intervention. The prophet wrote, *"He was wounded for our transgressions. He was bruised for our iniquities. The chastisement of our peace was upon Him and by His stripes are we made whole."* As Church Through the Roof, let's use what we go through to help someone get through.

QUESTIONS FOR GROUP DISCUSSION

1. Discuss our normal responses to conflict.
2. How has unresolved conflict impacted your life? The community? The church?
3. Discuss ways in which God has been marginalized.
4. What are your thoughts on the author's acronym HEALTH as a tool for conflict?
5. What have been your major challenges for dealing with conflict?

10

CHANGE

TEXT: *"When Jesus saw their faith, He said to the paralytic, 'Son, your sins are forgiven you.' And when some of the scribes were sitting there and reasoning in their hearts, 'Why does this Man speak blasphemies like this? Who can forgive sins but God alone?' But immediately, when Jesus perceived in His spirit that they reasoned thus within themselves, He said to them, 'Why do you reason about these things in your hearts? Which is easier, to say, "Your sins are forgiven you," or to say, "Arise, take up your bed and walk?" But that you may know that the Son of Man has power on earth to forgive sins'—He said to the paralytic, 'I say to you, arise, take up your bed and go to your house.' Immediately he arose, took up the bed, and went out in the presence of them all, so that all were amazed and glorified God, saying, 'We never saw anything like this before!'" (Mark 2:5–12, NKJV)*

"The world as we have created it is a process of our thinking. It cannot be changed without changing our thinking." Albert Einstein

Our Spiritual Renewal preacher, Dr. E. L. Branch, would probably begin this sermon by asking, "What would your life be like if you were known more by your condition than your name? Who would you be if your condition defined you? How would you feel if everyone you met identified you by what limited you rather than what you could potentially be?" Many people, even now, are known more by their condition than anything else. With all of the outrage and uproar in our country, Michael Brown, Trayvon Martin, and Tamir Rice are known mostly as unarmed black teenagers shot down by white police. None are known by what they could have been.

Consider the catalyst character of our text: the paralytic. He is presented in the Bible as a paralytic. We are just told he was paralyzed. Please note that unlike the woman with an issue of blood for twelve years, and the man by the pool for thirty-eight years, or the bent over sister of eighteen years, we are not told how long the man had been paralyzed. If we were to provide a biographical sketch, it would have only two words: The Paralytic. It's possible his paralysis could have been from birth or the result of some illness or calamity. We are only told he was paralyzed, which seems to have been for so long that he was identified as the paralytic. In other words, his condition defined him. Tragically, he's not identified by name, family, or community. He is identified simply as the paralytic.

The text says the men carried the paralytic. The text says Jesus spoke to the paralytic. However, something brought the man to a place where being paralyzed was not the way he wanted to live or be remembered. Perhaps the change he witnessed in his comrades awakened something within him that gave him hope for something different. Something changed in his thinking about himself, so he sought to change who he was. George Bernard Shaw once said, **"Those who cannot change their minds cannot change anything."** The man no longer wanted to live out his life branded as a paralytic. He no longer wanted to be defined by his condition, so he collaborated with some compassionate brothers and creatively sought to do something different with his life. He, along with his fellow brethren, believed that if he could get to Jesus, change was possible.

We Christians claim that the presence of Jesus makes the difference. All of us who truly embrace the saving grace of God in Jesus Christ have wholeheartedly purported and reported that Jesus made the difference. Before we ever raised the banner of Church Through the Roof, we touted and shouted of the difference Jesus made in our lives. I can truly join with the songwriter that my life has never been the same since Jesus came into my life. It's scary to think about, and should frighten all who know me, what my life would be like without Jesus. My identity would be something totally different than it is if not for the change wrought in me by Jesus. My personality, my emotionality, my psyche, perhaps even my appearance would be different if not for the change Jesus has made in my life. I admit and submit that my journey with the Lord didn't start like this, but I've found a way to include Jesus in every aspect of my life, and oh what a difference it makes. If not for Jesus, I too would probably be known more from my condition than anything else.

I must bring again to your attention that Church Through the Roof is a witness in the world that does whatever is necessary to get people to Jesus. It does church differently because we are energized by the reality that Jesus is in the house. Secondly, because Jesus is in the house, people are welcomed and accepted just the way they are. Thirdly, because Jesus is in the house, a healing word is preached and taught. Church Through the Roof is an approach to ministry that emphasizes the presence of Jesus, the acceptance of people, and where a healing word is being proclaimed. The end result of such a triune emphasis is that not only are lives changed, but even the community and institutions are changed. Nothing ought to stay the way it is while in the presence of the Lord, not even the church or a denomination.

> **A marginalized God skews, twists, and distorts our relationship with people and how we approach ministry.**

I reiterate this truth because of something I noted in the previous chapter. I noted that our text not only revealed how we marginalize people, it also revealed how we marginalize God. A marginalized God skews, twists, and distorts our relationship with people and how we approach ministry. In our text, Jesus was in the house, but the most influential people in the house wanted things to remain the same. In fact, their reasoning concluded that Jesus's words of acceptance and forgiveness were antithetical to the dominant claims of the house. They said, *"Only God forgives sins."* A marginalized God takes place when a community, institution, or church struggles with manifesting the presence of God by extending forgiveness and infusing new life. A marginalized God is pushed aside, and a community, institution, or church remains stagnant while advertising that Jesus is in the midst. No institution, community, or church should ever remain the same when Jesus is present. The only way a church remains the same with Jesus in the house is that the church has marginalized Jesus to the status of just being a token, or a marketing ploy to attract "weakly" customers.

This chapter addresses another one of those difficult subjects for communities, institutions, people, and yes, the church, which is the issue of change. The issue of change is a challenging, even difficult, concept for most of us. As eager and progressive as we might claim to be, most of us struggle with issues of change. For instance, seven years ago, Barak Obama became the first African American president, but the US Senate and most of Congress remained old, male, and white. The presidential campaign being held seven years later is mostly old, white, and male. Leadership in most black churches remains male, even with more black women in seminary than black males. The reason most of our churches are the way they are is because the issue of change is an unwelcomed and harshly resisted concept.

I want to challenge us to see beyond the picture we shape of this text when viewed through Western/American eyes. Western eyes view this text and see the change of an individual, the paralytic man. Such a hermeneutic limits the power of God as being concerned only with individuals. However, such is never the intention of the biblical text, or of biblical faith. Jesus did not come to save just individuals. The Bible says he came to save His people. He came to save a community from the oppressive powers of sin and evil. The most obvious evil in Jesus's day was not individual failure, but the failure of a community to live out their God-given privileges, largely because of succumbing to the oppressive regime of the Roman Empire. The early church did not view itself as concerned only with individuals, but with the community, the people of God. In fact, the early church was persecuted because they ***"had all things in common"*** and for ***"turning the world upside down."*** Church persecution was the result of violent resistance to community change.

Consider the fact that the paralytic man represents a symbol of a paralyzed people, people limited by an internalized definition of who they were. The attraction of Jesus was that He brought a healing word, a word of authority, unlike the scribes. The change we need is not just in individuals. We need change in society, change in the country, and yes, change in the church. Church Through the Roof is about a change in how we do church so that changed people are truly changed and supported in their change. How can lives be changed if the church remains the same? If we want to see something different, we have to be something different.

Change doesn't mean the people who went before us haven't done anything. Bishop Joseph Walker aptly states, "We'll never make our destiny by forgetting our history." I believe there's a word for change that might help us at this juncture. The word is "alter." Alter means to make something different without changing it into something else. The man's condition was changed, but he was the same man. He was the same man who was lowered into the house, but he walked out to live in the world a different way. I want to use the word **ALTER** as an acronym to help us hear the text.

A – Acts of faith
L – Liberating realities
T – Triggers controversy

E – Experience of love

R – Response to God's Word

First of all, Church Through the Roof embodies change whenever and wherever there are acts of faith. The text says, *"When Jesus saw their faith."* Change is a response to acts of faith. Jesus helps us see that faith is not an abstract concept wrapped in pious phrases, doctrinalized, or marginalized in religiosity. Faith, according to our text, was a lived activity. Jesus saw it. Jesus saw people who put some skin in the game. Faith is a lived experience. Faith is what we do to bring about what we hope for. *"Faith is the substance of things hoped for, the evidence of things not seen."*

In a recent visit to our church, the Reverend Jesse Jackson noted that faith is the substance, not the hope, but the manifestation of the hope. For too long, faith has been gutted of its substance by marginalized systems of beliefs and doctrines.

We marginalize God when we reduce faith to a system of beliefs that produces no actions. I weary of people telling me they have faith, but never do anything. We don't possess faith. Faith possesses us. When possessed by faith, we seek that which is not present and go for that which we desire. That's why the Bible says, *"We walk by faith, and not sight."* Our churches embody Church Through the Roof when the minority of us quit looking at what the majority is not doing and start doing what the majority should be doing. Faith is minorities acting like majorities.

> Change takes place when people make their faith visible for not only God to see, but for the world to see.

All it took was four men carrying a pallet, and one man on the pallet, to put the pallet out of business, precipitate a move of God, and alter the house. All it takes is a small group of us to act on what we believe is possible and we will show the world that with God all things are possible. Change takes place when people make their faith visible for not only God to see, but for the world to see.

Change is not only embodied in acts of faith, **but change is a liberating reality.** *"When Jesus saw their faith, He said to the paralytic, 'Son, your sins are forgiven you.'"* The idea of forgiveness is an economic term that declares a person free from debt. The Lord's Prayer makes that point when it says, *"And forgive us our debts, as we forgive our debtors."*

Change is a liberating reality. When someone or an institution is set free from that which has held it in bondage, the person or the institution is empowered to live life in a new way. So many people are paralyzed because what they once did won't let them go. An unforgiving spirit is a bound, captive, and imprisoned spirit. Churches are known to be in a state of paralysis because the things they used to do won't let them go. As a nation, we might truly be able to sing, "My country 'tis of thee, sweet land of liberty" if our pathological "isms" became what Frederick D. Haynes III, calls "wasms." Paul wrote, *"If any man be in Christ (which is to be an active recipient of His forgiveness), old things pass away. Behold, all things have become new."* You want to be free? Change! You want to see your church free in the Lord? Change! *"Where the spirit of the Lord is there is liberty."* Our forebears would say that when we experience God's forgiveness and look at our hands, they'll look new, and look at our feet, and they will too.

Change never comes without controversy. The reason why so many of us feel paralyzed in unhealthy lifestyles is because our minds won't let us change. Our minds rebel against our best intentions. My dear friend Reverend Dr. James Thomas of Saint Paul, Minnesota has inferred that we have been known to vote against our best interests. **Change triggers controversy.** We noted in the previous chapter, and it's still in the text, that the gatekeepers of religious and social tradition were appalled by the audacity of Jesus to be setting people free. *"Who can forgive sins but God alone?"*

Perhaps the litmus test of change could be determined by how many people our change upsets. There are some people who would rather we remain bound, enslaved, and defined by what's wrong with us than for us to be loosed, liberated, and living life in a new way. Too many of us have been duped into thinking that the church is fine just the way it is, with an aging population, no babies being born, and very few young, professional families in our midst. Change that brings out the best in some people will also bring out the worst in some people. If it happened to Jesus, it will also happen to us. Start altering the way people live in the world, and it will trigger controversy.

Change is also **an experience of love.** In that great chapter of love, 1 Corinthians 13, Paul speaks of, *"Faith, hope, and love, these three, but the greatest of these is love."* When it comes to changes wrought by God, such changes are experiences of love. Love brought the man before Jesus, and love moved Jesus to change his situation. Jesus said, ***"'But that you may know that the Son of Man has power on earth to forgive sins,' He said to the paralytic, 'Arise, take up your bed and go to your house.'"*** Jesus loved so deeply that He did not allow the adoring crowd to compromise Him. He did not allow controversy to impede the acts of faith. Jesus seized the opportunity to change the man's situation just by loving Him into a new way of living.

Forgiveness is not only liberating, it's also loving. Someone has said, ***"There are not five or six wonders of the world, but only one alone: love."*** Some of us have an opportunity to change things just by allowing people to experience our love. God has blessed us with the church that gives us as an opportunity to love one another beyond our socially paralyzing conditions. The church has always consisted of people with competing personalities to challenge us to love. Like the paralytic, there are so many people who will never get up from where they are, or being who they are, unless they experience love. Dionne Warwick was right when she sang,

> **The church needs to quit trying to fix and change people. Only God can change people.**

What the world needs now is love sweet love,
It's the only thing that there's just too little of.
What the world needs now is love sweet love,
No not just for some, but for everyone.

The church needs to quit trying to fix and change people. Only God can change people. What we can do is love the hell out of people. If we love people, they will change and become what God intends for them to become. Let us just love, and God will fix who needs to be fixed.

Finally, **change is a natural response to God's Word.** Notice in our text, Jesus does not touch the man. There is no anointing of oil. He does not tell the man to go and dip in a pool or go before the priest. The Bible shows us that Jesus just spoke the Word. In fact, this entire pericope is energized by the Word. The house filled up because ***"it was heard that He was in the house."*** The people gathered and blocked the door, ***"And He preached the word to them."*** He saw their faith. He spoke words of forgiveness. The controversy of

> **Disobedience paralyzes people and paralyzes the church.**

the scribes was resolved by the Word when Jesus asked, *"Which is easier, to say to the paralytic, 'Your sins are forgiven you,' or to say, 'Arise, take up your bed and walk?' He said to the paralytic, 'I say to you, arise, take up your bed and walk.'"*

Everything happens because of what Jesus said. Every action and reaction is in response to what Jesus said. But please note the man's response to Jesus's words. He *"arose, took up the bed, and went out in the presence of them all."* In other words, the paralyzed man became a walking man because he responded to God's Word. The bed-bound man became a bed-toting man because He responded to God's Word. Responding to God's Word is called "obedience." He obeyed himself into a change.

I'm too close to not see it and too moved to not say it. Perhaps his paralytic condition was like so many of ours—he suffered from the paralysis of disobedience. Disobedience paralyzes people and paralyzes the church. Some of us have some stuff in our lives that's not going anywhere until we obey God's Word. Some of us will always be what we've always been because we refuse to obey God's Word. Our church will miss its moment of change if it fails to obey God's Word.

I remember getting upset with someone I should have loved and wanted to maintain my self-justified position of anger. A dear friend patiently and lovingly listened to my story and told me if my outlook and position was to change, I needed to give God something to work with. I needed to forgive this person like I know God has forgiven me. I needed to respond to the radical word of forgiveness that God had given me and give it to someone else.

Jesus spoke and the man responded. He rose up, picked up his bed, and walked. He did everything the Lord told him to do. He didn't modify the Word to make himself comfortable in paralysis. He rose up, he took up, and he went out. He rose up and he took up. Church Through the Roof rises up and takes up.

Church Through the Roof is change from just church going to church being. Church Through the Roof is a radical change from having the church to becoming the church. It's a response to God's Word. We rise up, we take up, and we walk. Church Through the Roof is a change from the paralysis of church membership to active discipleship, because disciples respond to God's Word by rising up and taking up. Church Through the Roof is a change from the paralysis of just being in the church to being active in the world, because God's Word said, *"Go into all the world and make disciples of all people (black people, white people, red people, yellow people, rich people, poor people, straight people, gay people)."*

We rise up, take up, and walk! Church Through the Roof is a change from the paralysis of holding down a position to doing ministry by rising up and taking up as a response to God's Word. Church Through the Roof is a change from the paralysis of sitting down on a pew to rising up and taking up by standing up for justice, standing up for freedom, and standing up for equality. Church Through the Roof is a change from just praising the Lord to rising up and taking up and serving the Lord in response to His word. Church Through the Roof obeys God's Word and rises up! Takes up! Rises up! Walks! Takes up! Rises up! Walks! Takes up! Rises up! Takes up! Walks!

QUESTIONS FOR GROUP DISCUSSION

1. Discuss some of the common responses to change.

2. In what ways have people's condition impacted their identity?

3. How have you responded to change in your life, world, family, and church?

4. What are your responses to the author's acronym ALTER as a healthy response to change?

5. What's in the way of your church experiencing life-giving change?

11

COMMISSION

TEXT: *"When Jesus saw their faith, He said to the paralytic, 'Son, your sins are forgiven you.' And when some of the scribes were sitting there and reasoning in their hearts, 'Why does this Man speak blasphemies like this? Who can forgive sins but God alone?' But immediately, when Jesus perceived in His spirit that they reasoned thus within themselves, He said to them, 'Why do you reason about these things in your hearts? Which is easier, to say, "Your sins are forgiven you," or to say, "Arise, take up your bed and walk?" But that you may know that the Son of Man has power on earth to forgive sins'—He said to the paralytic, 'I say to you, arise, take up your bed and go to your house.' Immediately he arose, took up the bed, and went out in the presence of them all, so that all were amazed and glorified God, saying, 'We never saw anything like this before!'" (Mark 2:5–12, NKJV)*

What is it about you that cannot be explained apart from God? Is there anything in your life that stands out as a distinct work of God? Are you willing to give God the opportunity to showcase your life for His cause? It should be noted that only what can be attributed exclusively to God is believable and everything else is suspect.

I want to believe that God has made a difference in our lives. I want to believe that when Jesus saved us, we were released to be someone other than who we were. I further want to believe that all we say about Jesus leads to us doing something for Jesus. There ought to be some marked and noted changes in who we are after Jesus versus who we were before Jesus.

Perhaps the paralytic of our text can help us think more deeply about what it means to have a life-changing encounter with Jesus. Here is man whose mission in life begins after God changes his station in life. A man known only as a paralytic is literally carried to Jesus, but walks out on a mission for Jesus. He couldn't even get to church through normal means, but he leaves church doing what church people are supposed to do, which is to do what Jesus commissions us to do. He came in lying down, but he went out standing up. He came in being carried on a bed. He went out carrying the bed. He came in needing a word. He went out obeying the word. He came in a project. He went out on assignment. He came in wanting to get to Jesus. He went out living for Jesus. A moment with Jesus empowered him to live a lifetime for Jesus.

I love this brother because he doesn't just get in position for God to change his life, but makes himself available so God can use his life. He doesn't just allow God to alter his life, but he gets involved in the life of God. We teach in Experiencing God that God is at work in the world, seeking a relationship with us that is real and personal, yet also inviting us to join God in His work. The once paralytic man is a work of God who becomes a co-laborer with God. He joins God in God's work. The change in his life became an opportunity to bring change to the world.

Church Through the Roof is about getting people to Jesus who will also be in mission with Jesus. Church Through the Roof is about people experiencing the life-changing power of God in such a way that they willingly become conduits of God's power. All it took was a Church Through the Roof experience to get him to become church in the world, beginning in his own home. All it took was for some compassionate brothers to creatively collaborate, and a changed brother became a responsible brother. The God who made a way for him began using him as a way to get others to God.

I was privileged to spend a significant part of my life in the South. I went to school in the South. Three of my children were born in the South. My first church was a Southern church. I was blessed to live in Nashville, the capital of denominational life. I discovered that most of our major denominations are headquartered in Nashville. While there, I ran across a group of people known as the Primitive Baptist. The Primitive Baptist represents a group of people who distinguish themselves from other Baptists by being anti-missionary. In the nineteenth century, a schism arose among Baptists over missions, thus creating what is now called Missionary Baptist. The Missionary Baptist grew while the Primitive Baptist declined.

We are known, chartered by the state, and tagged in name as the Bethlehem Missionary Baptist Church. By name and affiliation, we are a pro-mission church. We are a people who claim to be on mission with God. The aim of this chapter represents a challenge for us to reclaim our missionary roots by reconnecting with our missionary God. We cannot be on mission for God without God. Whenever we try to do missions without God, we not only run the risk of marginalizing God, we also risk marginalizing the church.

I have been proposing that a marginalized God skews, twists, and distorts how we view people and how we do church. Likewise, a marginalized church

> A marginalized church distances itself from both God and the people who need God the most.

skews, twists, and distorts how we do ministry. A marginalized church distances itself from both God and the people who need God the most. A marginalized church goes where it wants to go and not where God commissions it to go. We want God to be where we want God to be rather than us being where God wants us to be. A marginalized church doesn't want to have anything to do with broken people because we really don't want to have anything to do with a God who welcomes, accepts, and mends broken people.

The truth is we can never do ministry for God without God. In fact, the word for doing ministry with God is not missions, but commission. We were not given a great mission. We were given a Great Commission, which says, ***"Go into all the world and make disciples, baptizing them in the name of the Father, the Son, and the Holy Spirit, teaching them to observe all things whatsoever I commanded you, and lo I will be with you always even to the end of the age."***

I pray you didn't miss it! It says, ***"whatsoever I commanded you, and lo I will be with you always..."*** Commission literally means, "to bring together." When living out the commission, we bring together what God could only do with people who have a need for God. We bring together our experiences with God in obedience to the Word of God. The man in our text was commissioned. Church Through the Roof is a commissioned church. It is a response to a God who brings our life-changing experiences together with God on God's mission.

I've got another word that can help us hear the text, as well as help us with our commission. The word comes from another Bible word, which is apostle. Apostle literally means, "sent one." The man, in obedience to Jesus's word, becomes a "sent one." He is apostolized. So I want to use the word **SENT**:

S – Source of God's power
E – Evidence of God's work
N – No excuses accepted
T – Target of God's concern

If we are not apostolized, we fossilize. If we are not being missionary, we are being stationary.

Church Through the Roof is made up of people who are sent. According to our text, the **commissioned are those who are willing to be sources of God's power.** Church Through the Roof is composed of people who hear Jesus when He says, *"I say to you, arise..."* Please note that the command of Jesus is directed to the paralytic, not the crowd, not the scribes, or the four men who carried him in. Jesus's command was to the one who most needed to be changed, not the crowd paralyzed in curiosity or the scribes paralyzed in their position and crippled by their ghettoized theology. He spoke to what we call in psychology the identified patient, the one who in fact is acting out the pathological condition of the community. He would be the one who would be used as a source of God's power. The Bible says, *"Immediately he arose..."* He obeyed Jesus's command and accepted God's commission.

Some of you can testify that you know in your heart your life was not changed until you heard the Lord speak directly to you and you decided to obey. People who represent the source of God's power do not obey through secondhand mediums, hand-me-down-testimonies, or grapevine confessions. They respond to God's Word directed to them. Some of you know you would still be paralyzed in some crippling pain, paralyzed in chronic confusion, hung up in a bad habit, paralyzed in toxic relationships, paralyzed in cycles of stupidity, if God had not spoken a life-changing word to you and you decided to obey. "I say to you, Alvin..." "I say to you, Marvin..." I say to you, Dewanda..." "I say to you, arise..." *"Arise"* is a word for "be enlivened." In essence, God said to us, "Be alive in a way you have never been! Make the power of God live in your life."

The commissioned of God are those who are willing to bring together the life God has enlivened in them so others may know that God lives. God lives in people who respond to God's Word. If you know that your life is because of God, then you are a source of God's power. Moreover, the only person you can count on God using is you. You are the source of God's deliverance for the people in your life. You are the source God wants to use to manifest His power in the world. God wants to use you to show the world what only God can do.

Jesus told the man, *"I say to you, arise, take up your bed..."* It was not enough for the man to be enlivened, but he also needed to be empowered. Jesus told him to pick up the very thing he had depended upon, and he did. **The commissioned are those who have been empowered to give evidence of God's work.** The bed carried by the man would be evidence for all to see that he could handle what once handled him. He carried what once was needed to carry him. He lifted up what once lifted him.

Perhaps some of you may not see the carrying of the bed as necessary. Try looking at the bed as evidence. The bed would serve as evidence for all to see what he used to be. Wherever he went, his bed would be with him. Whoever saw him would see his bed. Whenever someone asked him, "What's that you are carrying? Why is it important?" he would be able to present the bed as evidence of God's work in his life. The bed also made him vulnerable, believable, and credible. I recall sharing my testimony of deliverance in a silk-stocking church in Washington, DC, and some resting-on-their-laurels, heaven-bound-and-no-earthly-good members called the pastor and complained. They were not comfortable with preachers being honest and vulnerable in the pulpit. They were OK with me being a graduate of Bishop College and Vanderbilt University, but they didn't want to hear about how I got there through drugs, crime, gang banging, and life-denying foolishness. The truth is that until we get to the place where we present evidence of how far the Lord has brought us, we are not truly believable.

Again, the necessity of our small groups becomes apparent. In small groups, people have greater opportunity to present their bed. Among people we feel safe with, we are more likely to take the risks of vulnerability and give credible evidence of how God has worked in our lives. The truth is all of us have a bed we've been hiding, and Church Through the Roof allows us to accept Jesus's commission and present evidence of how God has worked in our life. In fact, I hold in suspicion a bed-less Christianity. I believe God has delivered all of us from something, and from someone, especially the demon of our self-illusions and delusions.

The immediate response of the man is noteworthy. The Bible says, **"Immediately he arose, took up the bed, and went out…"** It appears that when Jesus spoke to the man, he had no option but to obey. He did not say, "I've been here so long that I've become comfortable." He did not say, "I see no need to change my way of living." He doesn't look for an excuse to continue living the way he had always lived. It looks like by the time he got to Jesus, he had run out of excuses. The young people would say he had "excused out." Benjamin Franklin once said, **"He that is good for making excuses is seldom good for anything else."**

Church Through the Roof consists of people who have no excuses. The commissioned are those who go forth with no excuses. We have no excuse for

> "You can make excuses or you can make progress, but you can't make both."

not doing what the Lord has told us to do. We have no excuse for not going where the Lord has told us to go. We have no excuse for not making ourselves available as sources of God's power and evidence of God's work. Someone has said, **"You can make excuses or you can make progress, but you can't make both."** We will either make excuses or we'll make progress, but we can't make both.

A challenge for every church leader and ministry leader is to go on an excuse fast. For thirty days, don't make an excuse for not being responsible for your ministry. For thirty days, don't make an excuse for not doing your best. A challenge for every member is for thirty days, don't make an excuse for not tithing, no excuses for not giving sacrificially, no excuses for not attending Bible Study, and no excuses for not being present for meaningful discipleship opportunities. For thirty days, don't make an excuse for not supporting the pastor and encouraging other members. When we rise above our excuses, we will rise.

Jesus told the man to go to his house. *"Arise, take up your bed and go to your house."* He wasn't telling him to go to a place of brick and mortar. He wasn't just telling him to go to a certain address. He was telling him to go to the people who knew him when he was paralyzed and let them see him walk. In other words, he was commissioned to a specific target. His house was the target of God's concern. **Church Through the Roof leaves the church and goes to the target of God's concern.**

If we really want to know who God is concerned about—leave church! God is concerned about the people who will most know whether or not God has done something in our lives. God is concerned about the people who know us, and we know them. God is concerned about the people who knew us then and who know us now. We can't fake out the folks at our houses. We can't come up in our houses and impress the home crowd with holy words and sanctified behavior. If we do, the people at our houses will see right through us.

I know we want to stay around the church and act holy. I know we prefer hanging around the affirming energy of the church, but to join God in God's work we have to go to the target of God's concern. We don't need to be going to other people's neighborhood, just start at our own house. Like the paralyzed man, there are some more paralyzed folks in our houses. Our houses manufacture paralyzed people. Our houses are paralytic factories. Our houses make it easy for people to be paralyzed. Our houses support paralytic situations.

Isn't it true that our own houses need our witness? Isn't it true that our own houses need our energy. Our houses need the evidence of God working in us. Our houses need a no excuses witness. Our houses need to know the people in them are the targets of God's concern. Our houses need to know that God loves the folks there just the way they are. Go to our own houses and tarry until we can say, *"For me and my house, we will serve the Lord."*

The people of my upbringing understood such a witness, so they sang:

This little light of mine, I'm going to let it shine.

All in my home, I'm going to let it shine.

Let it shine. Let it shine. Let it shine.

QUESTIONS FOR GROUP DISCUSSION

1. Ask someone in the group to identify something about you that cannot be explained apart from God.

2. Share with someone something you know about him or her that cannot be explained apart from God.

3. Do you feel a sense of obligation to share with others what God has done for you?

4. What are your thoughts on the author's acronym SENT?

5. What is in the way of you living out the Great Commission?

12

CELEBRATION

TEXT: *"When Jesus saw their faith, He said to the paralytic, 'Son, your sins are forgiven you.' And when some of the scribes were sitting there and reasoning in their hearts, 'Why does this Man speak blasphemies like this? Who can forgive sins but God alone?' But immediately, when Jesus perceived in His spirit that they reasoned thus within themselves, He said to them, 'Why do you reason about these things in your hearts? Which is easier, to say, "Your sins are forgiven you," or to say, "Arise, take up your bed and walk?' But that you may know that the Son of Man has power on earth to forgive sins"—He said to the paralytic, 'I say to you, arise, take up your bed and go to your house.' Immediately he arose, took up the bed, and went out in the presence of them all, so that all were amazed and glorified God, saying, 'We never saw anything like this before!'" (Mark 2:5–12, NKJV)*

Recently, we just completed a rather intense season of holidays. Holidays were just rolling one after another. There was Thanksgiving, Hanukkah, Christmas, Kwanza, and then New Year's celebrations. In early January, I was in the store and Valentine's cards were already on display. (Valentine's Day actually comes after the celebration of Martin Luther King Jr.'s birthday.) In the midst of all the scheduled holidays, there were birthdays, anniversaries, and even a few funerals that were labeled as celebrations of life.

I suspect most of us know something about being holiday weary. But when we consider all the other things that went on at the same time of the holidays, we might want a few more things to celebrate. For every birthday there was a murder. For every child born there was a suicide. For all of the good things that lifted us up, something happened to bring someone down. There were suicide bombers, terrorist threats and acts, plane crashes, accidents of all stripes, sicknesses, and a mass array of human discontent. In the midst of Christmas with my wonderful son, I got a letter from the IRS that I refused to open during the celebrations. I know I will have to face its burdensome news, but I was intentional about not sabotaging moments of celebration with words of painful disruption.

As we look further into our text, we see that Church Through the Roof encouraged and embraced celebrations. As attentive as the people were to the word bring preached and taught, when a paralyzed man jumped out of his bed

> Celebration has the power to move the most stubborn, inspire the most resistant, lift up the most troubled, and transform the most difficult.

and started walking, joyous celebration broke out. Everyone saw how he came in, and everyone saw how he went out, and that was cause for celebration. In fact, the text says, *"All were amazed and glorified God."* Even Jesus's enemies didn't miss the opportunity to celebrate.

Although not everyone was glad to see the man get up, there was no way in the world the people in that space were going to let a few grouches sabotage the moment for celebration. Celebration has the power to move the most stubborn, inspire the most resistant, lift up the most troubled, and transform the most difficult. There's something absolutely transformative about celebration, because it's hard to stay the way you are when everyone else is celebrating.

I believe we strengthen our witness as Church Through the Roof when we seize moments to celebrate. I've listened across the years to how irrelevant the church is, and I even made that declaration myself on more than one occasion. However, the witness of this text provides for us a way in which we can remain relevant. In her insightful book, *Relevance: The Power to Change Minds and Behavior and Stay Ahead of the Competition,* Andrea Coville cites that there are three dimensions to relevance: context, content, and contact.[29] When we consider our context, content, and contact, we can remain relevant, and there will always be something to celebrate. We not only have our stated and scheduled holidays, but there's always a birthday. Someone was born on each day of the year, even on a leap year. The other day, I saw a man who was born on the first day of the year who married a woman born on the first day of the year, and they had a baby born on the first day of the year.

We are not having as many as we would like to have, but there's always a marriage to celebrate, a promotion to celebrate, a graduation, or a dedication. Thomas J. Peters once said, *"Celebrate what you want to see more of."* If we want to see more healings, let's celebrate healing. If we want to see more

---

[29] Andrea Coville, *Relevance: The Power to Change Minds and Behavior and Stay Ahead of the Competition* (Brookline, MA: Bibliomotion, Inc., 2014), 64–77.

people in love, let's celebrate love. If we want to see more people recover from the death of loved ones, divorces, drugs, or disease, let's celebrate recovery. If we want to see more people saved and lives turned around, let's celebrate salvation. Let's celebrate turned around lives.

We just passed a law that will release a lot of brothers and sisters from prison. Perhaps we might see more formerly incarcerated brothers and sisters coming our way if we started celebrating brothers and sisters being liberated from one of the most dehumanizing experiences on the planet. I want our church to be the first church to start staging Celebrate Coming Home Day. That's in the Bible. Read Luke 4:18. It says, ***"To proclaim liberty to the captives."*** Such a celebration might free some brother or sister from the shameful stigmatization of having been incarcerated. Truth be told, all of us have a family member somewhere, at some time, who was incarcerated. If we took Jesus seriously and considered our context, content, and contacts, we would be having a whole lot of celebrations with the many marginalized brothers and sisters of our community who are poor, brokenhearted, oppressed, gay, homeless, jobless, hopeless, and helpless. Let's celebrate what we want to see more of.

The Jewish scholar, author, and prophet Abraham Heschel once noted that the reason we are not celebrating is because we've been seduced into being entertained. He noted that, "Instead of celebrating, we seek to be amused or entertained. Celebration is an active state, an act of expressing reverence or appreciation. To be entertained is a passive state—it is to receive pleasure afforded by an amusing act or spectacle. (Entertainment is resignation.) Celebration is a confrontation." Celebrating is giving attention to the transcendent meaning of life's activities.

When we first started on this text, I never saw it going this far, but the Lord kept showing us something else. The Lord especially wanted us to see that the man didn't get out of the house before a celebration took place. They didn't wait until they got home to talk, text, tweet, YouTube, or Facebook (oh, they didn't have those media capacities), but they broke out in the moment and glorified God. Join me once again as I pull out of this text another acronym to help us hear another vital dimension of Church Through the Roof. I want to use the word **GLORY** as a powerful expression of celebration. Let me first say something about the word "glory." The word is used to describe the brilliance of those who share or participate in that which only God can do. To "give glory to God" means to live and speak sincerely and from the heart about God's amazing nature or deeds—in such a way that we seek to do justice to the reality of who God is. We do well to create more opportunities to say "Glory!"

As an acronym for celebration, we offer the following:

G – God's activity
L – Lived out
O – Obviously special
R – Real time
Y – You are impacted

The first thing we notice in the text is that they glorified God. What God worked through Jesus was not about Jesus. It was not about the man. It was not about the four who helped to bring the man to Jesus. Everybody in the house, including Jesus's enemies, knew that what had taken place before them was a God activity. **Celebration is an experience of God's activity.**

I'm about to date myself. I remember when black people on TV were few and none. We could look at our black and white television for a whole week and not see one black face. I do remember a few, one of which was Pearl Bailey. Pearl Bailey once said, **"People see God every day, they just don't recognize him."** Perhaps the devil has paralyzed the church's capacity to engage in meaningful celebrations because we refuse to see what God is doing. We can't recognize the activity of God because we think our lives are being determined by what we are doing. We are spiritually paralyzed when the world starts orbiting around us.

Church Through the Roof is open to celebration because it stays on the alert for what God is doing. We teach that God is always at work around us; well, let's celebrate what God is doing. God's activities are not hard to find. Every day the sun comes up, new life is made possible. Every night the sun goes down, new life is being generated. We are blessed with a day and graced with a night because days and nights are the Lord's doing. That's why the psalmist declared, *"This is the day the Lord has made, let us rejoice and be glad in it."* Whatever God does in a day, or allows to pass in the night, let's celebrate! Church Through the Roof celebrates the wondrous works of God because we know God is always at work.

The Bible tells us what amazed them was that the *"man arose, took up his bed, and went out in the presence of them all."* The celebration that ensued was the result of a lived out experience. The man lived out what God was working out in his life. Everything Jesus told the man to do, he lived it out. Jesus told the man to arise. He arose. Jesus told the man to take up his bed. He took up his bed. Jesus told the man to go home, and he obeyed Jesus's command to go home. **Celebrations are lived experiences.**

> Happiness lives wherever we live. It lives in our relationships, in our families, in our responsibilities, one to the other.

Perhaps many of us are missing out on celebration because we are missing out on life. Rabbi Sacks noted that the reason many of us are missing out on life is because we don't recognize where happiness lives. Happiness lives wherever we live. It lives in our relationships, in our families, in our responsibilities, one to the other. There is no greater happiness than our relationship with God. Jesus sent the man home because that's where his happiness was going to be found—where he lived!

Church Through the Roof helps people celebrate lived experiences. I've been black all my life, and I know what black people have to live through. There ought never be a Sunday where someone doesn't start the celebration because of what we live through. There's no party like a Holy Ghost party when you celebrate what the Lord has done. No wonder the psalmist declared, *"Make a joyful noise unto the Lord, all you lands. Serve the Lord with gladness, come before His presence with singing."* Whatever the Lord has done for you is a lived experience.

The crowd celebrated the man's lived experience and they were all amazed. They were amazed because what had happened was obviously special. The man came in being carried and went out walking. He came in needing help, but went out going to help. He came in in need of service, but went out in service. **Celebrations are responses to what is obviously special.**

I have been lifting up young people throughout my ministry. If I catch a hint of a young person trying to do something with his or her life, I'm going to lift him or her up. I do it because I know what it means to overcome serious challenges and somehow make it through school. I know because of my own struggles and challenges. I want our young people to know that what they are doing is obviously special. When over 50 percent of our young people never graduate, only about 25 percent ever enroll in college, and only about 10 percent get a college degree, I know going to college is special.

When over 50 percent of all Christian marriages end in divorce, and over 65 percent of our children will spend most of their lives in single-parent homes, let's celebrate marriages because most of our marriages will not last. Let's celebrate family!

Let's celebrate any achievement because they are obviously special. Let's celebrate the things of God that amaze and astound us, because so much of what God is doing in our lives is obviously special. When I see Khalin Freeman[30] blow his horn with such love and passion, I rejoice, because in a day when young men are trying to blow one another's brains out, he's blowing a horn—that is obviously special!

They were amazed because what was going on was happening in real time. Here were a people who had stories of Moses crossing the Red Sea, stories of Joshua bringing down the walls of Jericho, stories of David slaying Goliath, stories of Deborah slaying the enemy, and stories of Esther saving her people. Yet here in their midst, they saw a paralyzed man get up and walk. They saw Jesus resist the status quo and speak words of forgiveness and new life into a man limited by station and circumstance. Like David slaying Goliath, they saw Jesus slay the stubborn assumptions of powerless religion. **Celebrations are experiences of real time.** Real time is a term to describe what's happening here and now.

I like nothing better than listening to my elders tell the stories of Jim Crow South and the amazing faith of our ancestors. I celebrate their journeys and praise God for each testimony. However, the people in Richmond in 2016 need the experiences of God in real time. I learned in this church the powerful meaning of **"Must Jesus bear this cross alone."** Dr. Newman would always point out, **"To serve this present age, my calling to fulfill"** is a declaration of real-time experiences with God. Some of you have been missing out on

---

[30] Khalin Freeman is a young man who joined us at seventeen years of age and plays an amazing saxophone.

celebrations by not sharing your real-time deliverances. Some of you have real-time demons the Lord has delivered you from. Some of you have real-time obstacles the Lord helped you overcome. Some of you have real-time screw-ups the Lord has helped you through. Some of you have real-time experiences with the Lord.

Finally, **celebrations are experiences where you are impacted.** They said, *"We never saw anything like this before."* They were so impacted by what they had experienced, they had to say something about it. The impact of the moment was so incredible, they could not hold their peace. The shouted in unison, *"We never saw anything like this before."*

The other week, I spoke with a woman who claimed she had gone to a school that I personally hold in disdain. I disdain the school because it has given people paper who have never written a paper. The school she attended has ruined a group of East Bay preachers by awarding them degrees without empowering them with actual learning. She had Doctor before her name and believed she was deserving of such a high academic honor. I asked her what was the one thing she learned as a result of her school experience. She answered, "I learned that God was in all things." I thought to myself she didn't have to go to school to learn that. She had a degree of no substance or impact.

Church Through the Roof promotes high impact experiences. If Jesus is in the house, His presence ought to have impact. If Jesus speaks a word, His word ought to have impact. If people are welcomed and accepted, such an experience ought to have impact. If compassionate people collaborate in creative ways, it ought to have impact. If conflict is dealt with in healthy ways, it ought to have impact. If people are commissioned to join God in God's work, the witness we provide ought to have impact. Likewise, the celebrations we have as the result of God moving in our lives ought to have impact.

Church Through the Roof celebrates the things that impact our lives. We celebrate those things that move us to give God glory. Isn't it interesting that what went on in the house was repeated on the cross? When Jesus was crucified, the Bible tells us that a soldier looking on couldn't help himself. He saw everything. He saw Jesus crucified. He saw Him nailed to the cross. He saw Him lifted high and stretched wide. He saw Him stripped and taunted by

His enemies, and heard Jesus say, ***"Father, forgive them for they know not what they do."*** On the cross, he saw Jesus speak words of love and new life. At a time when Jewish life didn't matter, he saw the sun dripped in blood. He felt the earth reel and rock, and he was so impacted, like Church Through the Roof, he glorified God and declared, ***"Surely this man is the Son of God!"***

If He's impacted your life, let's celebrate by saying so!

QUESTIONS FOR GROUP DISCUSSION

1. Discuss and assess the meaning of the prominent celebrations within the life of your church, family, and community.

2. List some of the things you and your church, family, and community want to see more of.

3. In what ways can you and your church, family, and community celebrate what you want to see more of?

4. What are your thoughts on the author's acronym, GLORY?

5. What's in the way of you and your church, family, and community providing more celebrations?

BMBC CORE VALUES

SAFE GROUP: We will all do our part to create an environment where everyone can be real, open and honest in their struggles and victories.

CONFIDENTIALITY: What is said in the group stays in the group.

LISTEN: let's value one another during the discussions by really listening to what is being shared. Try to avoid thinking how you are going to respond or what you are going to say next.

PAUSE: Allow a pause in conversation after someone shares to give the person sharing the chance to finish and the group the opportunity to consider what was just shared before responding.

SILENCE: it is important to allow silence on the group as it provides an opportunity for someone to share and for members in the group to process the topic or question being considered.

NO "CROSS TALK": Be considerate of others as they are sharing. No side conversations.

NO FIXING: We are not here to fix each other. Jesus does that part. Give encouragement; speak truth and point to Jesus. Don't try to solve of fix each other.

NO RESCUING: When people are sharing something deeply personal, there can be a tendency to try to make them feel better about themselves or the situation by providing immediate condolences. This will often cause them to stop sharing. Resist the temptation to rescue people.

SHARING: Be sensitive about the amount of time you share.

BE SELF-AWARE: Be self-aware of how you are personally effecting the environment through your words, actions and non-verbal communications.

USE "I" STATEMENT: It's easy to talk about the issues of others, but for our purposes, we want you to put yourself on the table. Try to use "I" statements rather than "them". "the church", "us", "we", etc.

CONFLICT: We will commit to resolve conflict biblically. When conflict or sin issues between group members arise, we want to make sure that we are honoring God and each other in the way we deal with issues.

THE DISCIPLESHIP PROCESS: The Wheel

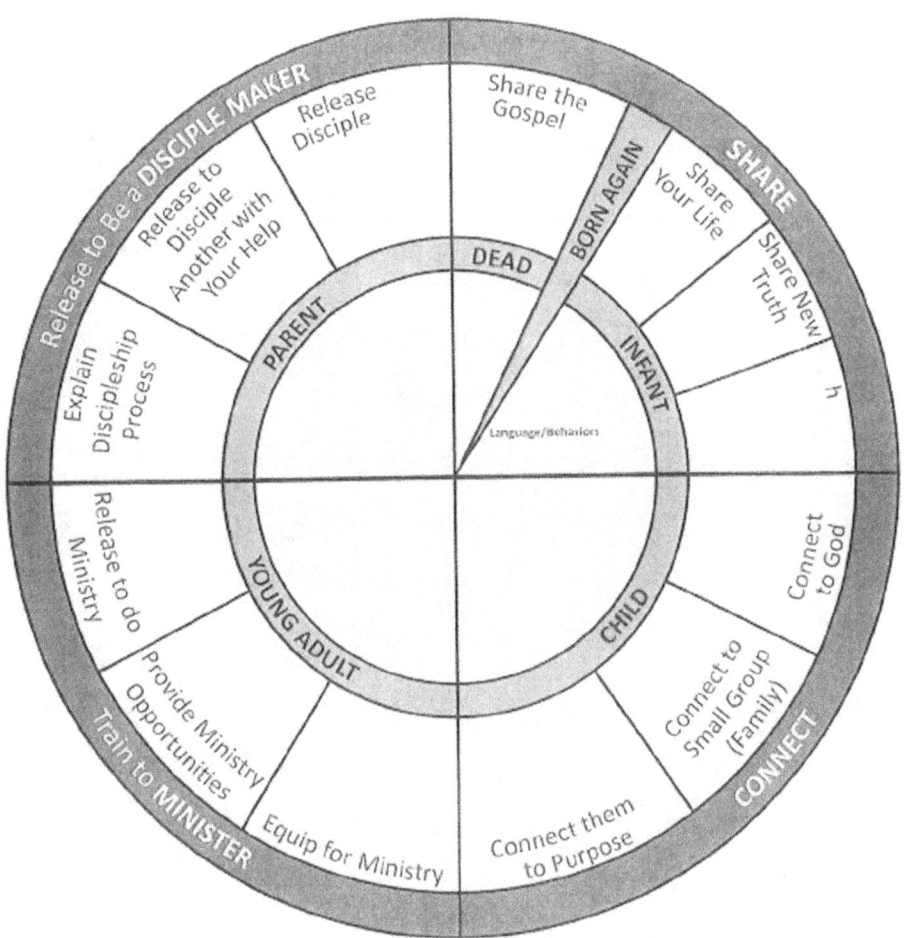

THE DISCIPLESHIP PROCESS: The 5 Stages Of Spiritual Growth
TRAITS, PHRASES & CHARACTERISTICS

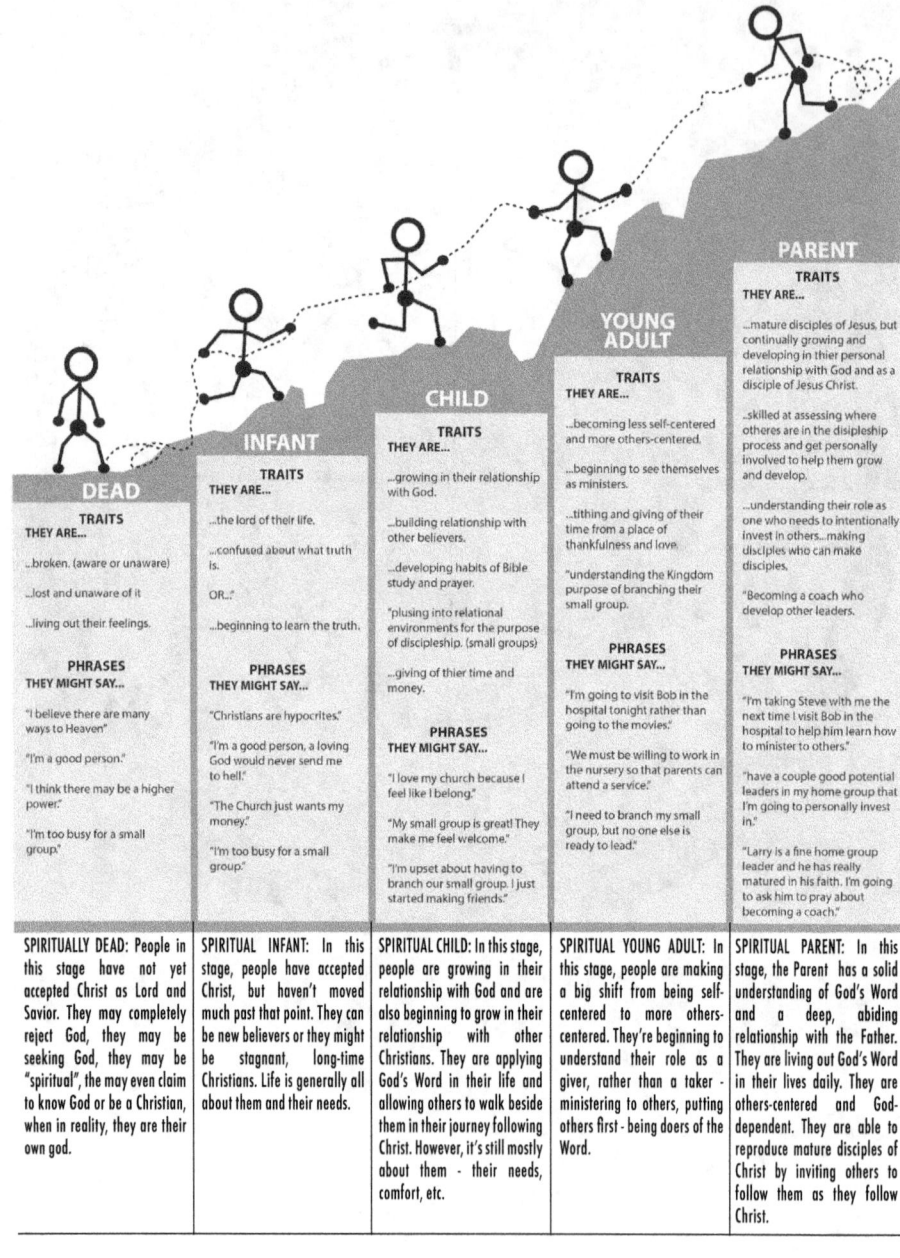

DEAD

TRAITS THEY ARE...
...broken. (aware or unaware)
...lost and unaware of it
...living out their feelings.

PHRASES THEY MIGHT SAY...
"I believe there are many ways to Heaven."
"I'm a good person."
"I think there may be a higher power."
"I'm too busy for a small group."

INFANT

TRAITS THEY ARE...
...the lord of their life.
...confused about what truth is.
OR...
...beginning to learn the truth.

PHRASES THEY MIGHT SAY...
"Christians are hypocrites."
"I'm a good person, a loving God would never send me to hell."
"The Church just wants my money."
"I'm too busy for a small group."

CHILD

TRAITS THEY ARE...
...growing in their relationship with God.
...building relationship with other believers.
...developing habits of Bible study and prayer.
"plusing into relational environments for the purpose of discipleship. (small groups)
...giving of thier time and money.

PHRASES THEY MIGHT SAY...
"I love my church because I feel like I belong."
"My small group is great! They make me feel welcome."
"I'm upset about having to branch our small group. I just started making friends."

YOUNG ADULT

TRAITS THEY ARE...
...becoming less self-centered and more others-centered.
...beginning to see themselves as ministers.
...tithing and giving of their time from a place of thankfulness and love.
"understanding the Kingdom purpose of branching their small group.

PHRASES THEY MIGHT SAY...
"I'm going to visit Bob in the hospital tonight rather than going to the movies."
"We must be willing to work in the nursery so that parents can attend a service."
"I need to branch my small group, but no one else is ready to lead."

PARENT

TRAITS THEY ARE...
...mature disciples of Jesus, but continually growing and developing in thier personal relationship with God and as a disciple of Jesus Christ.
...skilled at assessing where otheres are in the disipleship process and get personally involved to help them grow and develop.
...understanding their role as one who needs to intentionally invest in others...making disciples who can make disciples.
"Becoming a coach who develop other leaders.

PHRASES THEY MIGHT SAY...
"I'm taking Steve with me the next time I visit Bob in the hospital to help him learn how to minister to others."
"have a couple good potential leaders in my home group that I'm going to personally invest in."
"Larry is a fine home group leader and he has really matured in his faith. I'm going to ask him to pray about becoming a coach."

SPIRITUALLY DEAD: People in this stage have not yet accepted Christ as Lord and Savior. They may completely reject God, they may be seeking God, they may be "spiritual", the may even claim to know God or be a Christian, when in reality, they are their own god.

SPIRITUAL INFANT: In this stage, people have accepted Christ, but haven't moved much past that point. They can be new believers or they might be stagnant, long-time Christians. Life is generally all about them and their needs.

SPIRITUAL CHILD: In this stage, people are growing in their relationship with God and are also beginning to grow in their relationship with other Christians. They are applying God's Word in their life and allowing others to walk beside them in their journey following Christ. However, it's still mostly about them - their needs, comfort, etc.

SPIRITUAL YOUNG ADULT: In this stage, people are making a big shift from being self-centered to more others-centered. They're beginning to understand their role as a giver, rather than a taker - ministering to others, putting others first - being doers of the Word.

SPIRITUAL PARENT: In this stage, the Parent has a solid understanding of God's Word and a deep, abiding relationship with the Father. They are living out God's Word in their lives daily. They are others-centered and God-dependent. They are able to reproduce mature disciples of Christ by inviting others to follow them as they follow Christ.

www.ingramcontent.com/pod-product-compliance
Lightning Source LLC
Chambersburg PA
CBHW050601300426
44112CB00013B/2013